D1429845

The Employee Assistance Treatment Planner

The Employee Assistance Treatment Planner

James M. Oher

Daniel J. Conti

Arthur E. Jongsma, Jr.

JOHN WILEY & SONS, INC.

New York • Chichester • Weinheim • Brisbane • Singapore • Toronto

Published by John Wiley & Sons, Inc.

Published simultaneously in Canada.

This publication is designed to provide accurate and authoritative information in regard to the subject matter covered. It is sold with the understanding that the publisher is not engaged in rendering professional services. If legal, accounting, medical, psychological or any other expert assistance is required, the services of a competent professional person should be sought.

All references to diagnostic codes and the entire content of Appendix B are used with permission from *Diagnostic and Statistical Manual of Mental Disorders, Fourth Edition,* 1994, Washington, D.C.: American Psychiatric Association.

Library of Congress Cataloging-in-Publication Data:

Oher, James M.
     The employee assistance treatment planner / James M. Oher,
   Daniel J. Conti, Arthur E. Jongsma, Jr.
            p.   cm.
     Includes bibliographical references.
     ISBN 0-471-24709-X (pbk. : alk. paper). — ISBN 0-471-24730-8
   (pbk./disk : alk. paper)
     1. Employee assistance programs.   2. Employees—Counseling of.
   3. Psychotherapy—Planning.   I. Conti, Daniel J.   II. Jongsma,
   Arthur E., 1943–   III. Title.
   HF5549.5.E42035   1998
   658.3'82—dc21   98-23046
                                                         CIP

Printed in the United States of America.

10 9 8 7 6 5 4 3 2 1

CONTENTS

The Employee
Assistance
Treatment
Planner

INTRODUCTION

Work organizations and the nature of work itself will be transformed as the demand for change continues throughout this decade. Partially as a response to this resulting disequilibrium, Employee Assistance Programs (EAPs) are increasingly being offered by workplaces throughout the world to attend to the emotional, social, and psychological needs of employees. Employee Assistance Services are workplace-focused mechanisms designed to identify and aid employees who need professional assistance with problems in living that frequently impair their job performance. These problems in living are often connected to alcohol and other drug use, or marital, emotional, familial, and other stressors.

EAP work requires a clarification and prioritization of the problems that the employee presents. This *Planner* helps the EAP counselor with these needs and addresses the causes of job performance problems with step-by-step suggestions on how to resolve them. The *Planner* also provides direction and focus for the referral to community resources that may be needed to comprehensively address the problem. It delineates how EAP professional intervention aims to restore an employee to full productivity by facilitating solutions to common problems facing today's working population.

The demand for accountability and precise documentation of service is a slowly growing requirement within the EAP profession. The Joint Commission on Accreditation of Healthcare Organizations (JCAHO) recently announced the inclusion of employee assistance program services as part of its accreditation process product. The two international EAP organizations, the Employee Assistance Professional Association (EAPA) and the Employee Assistance Society of North America (EASNA), have set standards of EAP practice that have guided service and have shaped much of the quality assurance activity within the field. However, the standards are broad and open to a wide range of interpretation. This is particularly the case regarding the actual clinical intervention work performed by the EAP counselor.

The interventions, objectives, goals, and definitions in this book shed light into the "black box" of what EAP counselors actually do—prepare and catalyze clients for change. This book focuses on specific problems that the EAP counselor encounters in daily practice. It behaviorally defines how support is engaged and given; how guidance, direction, and focus are provided; and how goal-setting is begun. In an incremental, clear, and logical fashion, it delineates what the EAP counselor does when addressing these issues as well as what is required of the employee on the path toward problem resolution.

This book is different from other treatment planners in the Practice Planner series. It is not focused exclusively on psychotherapy. The EAP counselor is often in the role of identifying and setting in motion treatment that may ultimately solve an acute or chronic life problem. The counselor is usually in the role of guide, or manager, of a life-change process, helping to coordinate, explain, and support ongoing treatment and interventions by other professionals. Assessment and triage are necessities in EAP work because frequently it is the EAP counselor who is first on the scene, identifying and labeling a problem and then recommending, convincing, or persuading the employee to take the next steps toward problem resolution.

It is also the EAP counselor's role to work with a broad array of other professionals to find the solution to the employee's problem: psychotherapists, physicians, human resource managers, job counselors, educators, community resources, and more. Consequently, this *Planner* contains less emphasis on the practice of psychotherapy and more emphasis on pragmatic steps of gathering correct diagnostic information and presenting a treatment/problem-resolution plan that the employee, as well as the workplace, will support. It contains direction for monitoring the progress of treatment and for one of the particular core competencies of EAP work, follow-up support.

This book helps EAP counselors define their primary role: to identify, assess, refer, and follow up. It aims to be practical, progressive, and problem-resolution focused. It answers the question, "How do EAPs resolve problems?" Implicit within and part of EAP work is the development of goals and strategies needed to resolve problems. There is an increased need for EAP counselors to produce an effective, clear problem resolution plan in a short time frame. However, many EAP counselors, as well as mental health clinicians who desire to perform EAP work, have little experience in EAP plan development. Our purpose in writing this book is to clarify, simplify, and accelerate the EAP planning process.

TREATMENT PLAN UTILITY

Detailed EAP plans can benefit the employee, EAP counselor, and community treatment provider as well as the overall EAP process. The process is served by a plan because it clarifies the issues that are the focus of the EAP intervention process. The plan is a guide that structures the focus of the intervention process. Because issues can change as the work progresses, the plan must be viewed as a dynamic document that can and must be updated to reflect any major change of problem, definition, goal, objective, or intervention.

Employees and EAP professionals benefit from plans because a plan forces both to think about outcomes and problem resolutions. Behaviorally stated, measurable objectives clearly focus the intervention endeavor. Clear objectives that can be formulated by the EAP counselor allow the employee to channel efforts into specific changes that will lead to the long-term goal of problem resolution. The EAP counselor is in an excellent position to follow up, to evaluate, and, ideally to ensure that those goals are being reached. The EAP counselor guides the client into treatment when appropriate. The EAP counselor can ensure that therapy is not a vague process where clients just talk honestly and openly about emotions and cognitions until they feel better. The employee and the EAP professional, in preparatory work, concentrate on specifically stated objectives that are achieved through the use of specific interventions.

HOW TO DEVELOP A TREATMENT PLAN

The process of developing a plan involves a logical series of steps that build on each other much like constructing a house. The foundation of any effective plan is the data gathered in a thorough biopsychosocial assessment. As the employee presents himself or herself, the EAP counselor must sensitively listen to and understand what the employee struggles with in terms of current stressors, emotional status, effects on job performance and home life, social network, physical health, coping skills, self-esteem, and so on. Assessment data may also be gathered from a social history, a clinical interview, and contact with the employee's significant others. The integration of the data by the EAP is critical for understanding the employee. Once the assessment is complete, use the following six specific steps for developing an effective treatment plan.

Step One: Problem Selection

Although the employee may discuss a variety of issues during the assessment, the EAP counselor must ferret out the most significant problems on which to focus the process. Usually, a primary problem will surface, and secondary problems may also be evident. Some other problems may have to be set aside as not urgent enough to require resolution at this time. An effective plan can only deal with a few selected problems or the intervention will lose its direction. This *Planner* offers 28 problems from which to select those that most accurately represent an employee's presenting issues.

As the problems to be selected become clear to the EAP counselor, it is important to include opinions from the client as to his or her prioritization of issues for which help is being sought. A client's motivation to participate in and cooperate with the process depends to some extent on the degree to which the intervention addresses the client's greatest needs.

Step Two: Problem Definition

Every problem presents itself in a unique way in each individual employee's life. Therefore, each problem that is selected for intervention requires a specific definition that relates how it is evidenced in the particular employee. When appropriate, the symptom pattern should be associated with diagnostic criteria and codes such as those found in the *Diagnostic and Statistical Manual* or the *International Classification of Diseases.* The *Employee Assistance Planner,* following the pattern established by DSM-IV, offers an array of such behaviorally specific problem statements to choose from; the prewritten definitions may serve as a model for your own personally crafted statements. You will find several behavior symptoms or syndromes listed that may characterize one of the 28 presenting problems.

Step Three: Goal Development

The next step in treatment plan development is that of setting broad goals for the resolution of the target problem. Goals need not be crafted in measurable terms, but can be global, long-term goals that indicate a desired positive outcome to the procedures. The *EAP Planner* suggests several possible goal statements for each problem, but one statement is all that is required in a plan.

Step Four: Objective Construction

In contrast to long-term goals, objectives must be stated in behaviorally measurable language. The point at which the employee has achieved the established objectives must be clear; therefore, vague, subjective objectives are not acceptable. It is our belief that review agencies (e.g.,

JCAHO) will insist that EAP outcomes as well as treatment outcomes need to be measurable. The objectives presented in this *Planner* are designed to meet this demand for accountability. Numerous alternatives are presented to allow construction of a variety of plan possibilities for the same presenting problems. The EAP counselor must exercise professional judgment as to which objectives are most appropriate for a given employee.

In essence, objectives can be thought of as a series of steps that, when completed, will result in the achievement of the long-term goal. There should be at least two objectives for each problem, but the EAP counselor may construct as many as are necessary for goal achievement. Target attainment dates should be listed for each objective. New objectives should be added to the plan as the individual progresses. When all the necessary objectives have been achieved, the employee should have resolved his or her target problem successfully.

Step Five: Intervention Creation

Interventions are the actions of the EAP counselor designed to help the employee achieve the objectives. There should be at least one intervention for every objective. If the employee does not accomplish the objective after the initial intervention, new interventions should be added to the plan. Interventions should be selected on the basis of the employee's needs and the counselor's full therapeutic repertoire. The *EAP Planner* contains suggestions from a broad range of therapeutic approaches, including cognitive, dynamic, behavioral, pharmacological, systems-oriented, and solution-focused interventions. Other interventions may be written by the counselor to reflect his/her own training and experience. The addition of new problems, definitions, goals, objectives, and interventions to those found in the *Planner* is encouraged because doing so adds to the database for future reference and use.

Step Six: Diagnosis Determination

When appropriate, the determination of an actual diagnosis is based on an evaluation of the employee's complete clinical presentation. The EAP counselor must compare the employee's behavioral, cognitive, emotional, and interpersonal symptoms to the criteria for diagnosis of a mental illness as described in DSM-IV. Careful assessment of behavioral indicators facilitates a more accurate diagnosis and more effective treatment planning.

HOW TO USE THIS PLANNER

Learning the skills of effective plan writing can be a tedious and difficult process for many counselors. *The EAP Treatment Planner* was developed as a tool to aid EAP professionals in quickly writing treatment plans that are clear, specific, and customized to the particular needs of each employee. Treatment plans should be developed by moving in turn through each of the following steps:

Step One: Choose one presenting problem from those identified in the assessment process. Locate the corresponding page number for that problem in *The EAP Treatment Planner*'s table of contents.

Step Two: Select two or three of the listed behavioral definitions and record them in the appropriate section on the treatment plan form.

Step Three: Select a single long-term goal and record it in the goals section of your treatment plan form.

Step Four: Review the listed objectives for this problem and select the ones clinically indicated for the client. Remember, it is recommended that at least two objectives be selected for each problem. Add a target date or the number of sessions allocated for the attainment of each objective.

Step Five: Choose relevant interventions. The numbers of the interventions most salient to each objective are listed in parentheses following the objective statement. Feel free to choose other interventions from the list or to add new interventions as needed in the space provided.

Step Six: When appropriate, DSM-IV diagnoses that are associated with the problem are listed at the end of each chapter. These diagnoses are meant to be suggestions for clinical consideration. Select a diagnosis listed or assign a more appropriate choice from the DSM-IV.

Following these steps will facilitate the development of complete, customized treatment plans ready for immediate implementation and presentation to the client. The final plan should resemble the format of the sample plan presented at the end of this Introduction.

ELECTRONIC TREATMENT PLANNING

As paperwork mounts, more and more counselors are turning to computerized record keeping. The presenting problems, goals, objectives, interventions, and diagnoses in *The EAP Treatment Planner* are available in electronic form as an add-on upgrade module to the popular software *TheraScribe 3.0 for Windows: The Computerized Assistant to Treatment Planning.* For more information on *TheraScribe* or *The EAP Treatment Planner* add-on module, call John Wiley & Sons at 1-800-879-4539 or mail in the information request coupon at the back of this book.

A WORD OF CAUTION

Whether using the print *Planner* or the electronic version, *TheraScribe 3.0,* it is critical to remember that effective treatment planning requires that each plan be tailored to the client's problems and needs. *Treatment plans should not be mass produced, even if clients have similar problems.* Each employee's strengths and weaknesses, unique stressors, social network, family circumstances, and interactional patterns *must* be considered in developing a treatment strategy. The clinically derived statements in this *Planner* can be combined in thousands of permutations to develop detailed treatment plans. In addition, readers are encouraged to add their own definitions, goals, objectives, and interventions to the existing samples.

In closing, it is our hope that this book can be used to mentor those who want to become EAP professionals. We are conceptualizing and clarifying an area of practice that we feel is relevant for all professionals in the EAP field.

Knowing that this book is in constant evolution, we welcome and look forward to your comments and suggestions for possible future editions.

EAP SAMPLE TREATMENT PLAN

Problem: Abusive Partner

Behavioral Definition

1. Self-report of being injured by a domestic partner coupled with feelings of fear and social withdrawal.
2. Bruises or physical complaints that give evidence of assault.

Long-term Goals

1. Terminate verbal and physical abuse of any kind.
2. Seek mental health treatment to build self-esteem, assertiveness, and the confidence to end the abusive relationship.

Short-term Objectives	Therapeutic Interventions
1. Identify the history, nature, frequency, and duration of the abuse.	1. Actively build the level of trust with the employee through consistent eye contact, active listening, and unconditional positive regard to facilitate employee's identification and expression of feelings. 2. Gather a history of abuse that has been endured in the current and previous relationships.
2. Identify and express the feelings associated with the abuse.	1. Explore, encourage, and support the employee in verbally expressing and clarifying his/her feelings associated with the abuse.
3. Terminate self-blame for the abuse and place responsibility on the perpetrator.	1. Decrease the employee's feelings of shame and guilt by affirming the perpetrator as being responsible for the abuse.

(Continued)

4. Agree to follow through with counseling to resolve the abusive situation.

2. Confront the employee about making excuses for the perpetrator's abuse, minimizing its impact, or accepting blame for it.

1. Refer employee to a mental health professional for evaluation as to the need for ongoing counseling or medication.

2. Meet with employee periodically to encourage follow-through with counseling treatment plan.

5. Report a decrease in abuse interactions at home and work.

1. Follow up with employee to see how his/her behavior has changed and how he/she is setting firm boundaries on no tolerance of abuse.

ABUSIVE PARTNER

BEHAVIORAL DEFINITIONS

1. Confirmed self-report or account by others of verbal and physical assault (e.g., hitting, kicking, slapping, or torture) by another adult.
2. Self-report of being injured by a domestic partner coupled with feelings of fear and social withdrawal.
3. Intermittent crying and/or outbursts of anger while talking with a domestic partner on the telephone or in person at the workplace.
4. Bruises or physical complaints that give evidence of assault.
5. Pronounced disturbance of mood and affect (e.g., frequent and prolonged periods of depression, irritability, anxiety, and apathetic withdrawal).
6. Self-reported feelings of fear when in contact with domestic partner.
7. Absence from work due to embarrassment concerning physical bruises and other indications of assault.

—. _____
   _____
—. _____
   _____
—. _____
   _____

LONG-TERM GOALS

1. Terminate verbal and physical abuse of any kind.
2. Draw comfort and support from healthy and positive relationships at work.
3. Resolve feelings of depression, fear, and social withdrawal.

4. Obtain support and encouragement from members of a peer group who have had similar abusive relationships.
5. Eliminate denial about the partner's responsibility for the abuse.
6. Seek mental health treatment to build self-esteem, assertiveness, and the confidence to end the abusive relationship.

___. _____

_____

___. _____

_____

___. _____

_____

SHORT-TERM OBJECTIVES

1. Give an accurate and emotionally honest description of the most current abuse and the reason for seeking assistance now. (1)
2. Identify the history, nature, frequency, and duration of the abuse. (2)
3. Identify and express the feelings associated with the abuse. (1, 2, 3, 4)
4. Describe any abuse that is inflicted on others in the house. (5, 6)
5. Sign release of information forms for mental health professional and/or supervisor. (7)
6. Terminate denial of the seriousness of the problem. (8)

THERAPEUTIC INTERVENTIONS

1. Actively build the level of trust with the employee through consistent eye contact, active listening, and unconditional positive regard to facilitate employee's identification and expression of feelings.
2. Gather a history of abuse that has been endured in the current and previous relationships.
3. Explore, encourage, and support the employee in verbally expressing and clarifying his/her feelings associated with the abuse.
4. Stabilize the employee's mood and decrease the emotional intensity connected to the abuse.
5. Explore whether any other members of the employee's household have also been

7. Express the guilt and shame that he/she feels concerning the abuse. (9, 10)

8. Terminate self-blame for the abuse and place responsibility on the perpetrator. (9, 10, 11)

9. Verbalize the way the abuse has impacted functioning at home and at work. (12)

10. Verbalize an understanding of how low self-esteem perpetuates a cycle of violence and victimization. (13)

11. Describe any role that substance abuse may play in the pattern of violence. (14)

12. Comply with a comprehensive physical evaluation to ensure that no serious injuries have been sustained. (15)

13. Cooperate with a comprehensive psychological evaluation. (16)

14. Agree to follow through with counseling to resolve the abusive situation. (16, 17)

15. Attend victim support groups. (18)

16. Read books regarding victims of abuse to increase self-understanding. (19)

17. Report on progress made in group and/or individual counseling. (20, 21, 22, 23)

abused and notify the police and/or criminal justice officials as appropriate.

6. Take necessary steps (e.g., removal of the employee and children from the home, notification of protective services and/or police) to protect employee and family members from future physical abuse.

7. Seek written and verbal permission from the employee to share information regarding the abuse with supervisor and health professionals as appropriate.

8. Confront and challenge denial within the employee's belief system regarding the seriousness of the abuse.

9. Explore employee's feelings of guilt, shame, and/or self-blame for the abuse.

10. Decrease the employee's feelings of shame and guilt by affirming the perpetrator as being responsible for the abuse.

11. Confront the employee about making excuses for the perpetrator's abuse, minimizing its impact, or accepting blame for it.

12. Explore the impact of the physical and verbal abuse on the employee's ability to function at work and at home.

18. Report a decrease in abuse interactions at home and work. (24)

___. _____

_____

___. _____

_____

___. _____

_____

13. Teach the employee how low self-esteem allows for a toleration of abuse and how abuse reinforces low self-esteem.

14. Evaluate the possible role of alcohol or other drug use/abuse in the pattern of violence.

15. Refer employee to a physician for a physical exam.

16. Refer employee to a mental health professional for evaluation as to the need for ongoing counseling or medication.

17. Meet with employee periodically to encourage follow-through with counseling treatment plan.

18. Refer employee to a victim support group with other adults to assist him/her in realizing that others share similar experiences.

19. Suggest employee read *The Courage to Heal* (Bass and Davis); *Betrayal of Innocence* (Forward and Buck); or *Outgrowing the Pain* (Gil).

20. Assist employee in evaluating the mental health treatment.

21. Challenge employee's resistance to the treatment plan.

22. Reinforce employee's positive statements about him/herself and the future.

23. With appropriate per-
mission, follow up with
mental health professional
to see how treatment is
progressing.

24. Follow up with employee to
see how his/her behavior
has changed and how
he/she is setting firm
boundaries on no tolerance
of abuse.

—. _____

_____

—. _____

_____

—. _____

_____

DIAGNOSTIC SUGGESTIONS

Axis I: 309.0   Adjustment Disorder with Depressed Mood
296.xx   Major Depression
300.4   Dysthymic Disorder
V61.1   Physical Abuse of Adult

_____   _____

Axis II: 301.83   Borderline Personality Disorder
301.6   Dependent Personality Disorder
799.9   Diagnosis Deferred on Axis II
V71.09   No Diagnosis on Axis II

_____   _____

_____   _____

ANGER MANAGEMENT

BEHAVIORAL DEFINITIONS

1. History of disciplinary actions in the workplace and/or career setbacks resulting from hostile interactions with coworkers or managers.
2. Hostile overreaction to insignificant irritants.
3. Swift and harsh judgment statements made to or about others.
4. Tense body language (e.g., clenched fist or jaw, glaring stares, or refusal to make eye contact) that intimidates or frightens others.
5. Use of passive-aggressive patterns (social withdrawal due to anger, lack of complete or timely compliance in following directions or rules, complaining about authority figures behind their backs, or failure to meet expected behavioral norms).
6. Consistent pattern of challenging or disrespectful treatment of managers.
7. Use of verbally abusive language.
8. Threats of harm to coworkers or the company.

—. _____
   _____
—. _____
   _____
—. _____
   _____

LONG-TERM GOALS

1. Decrease overall intensity and frequency of angry feelings and increase ability to recognize and appropriately express angry feelings as they occur.

2. Develop awareness of current angry behaviors, clarifying origins of and alternatives to aggressive anger.
3. Come to an awareness and acceptance of angry feelings while developing better control and more serenity.

—. _____

_____

—. _____

_____

—. _____

_____

SHORT-TERM OBJECTIVES

1. Verbalize angry feelings and the targets of and causes for those feelings, especially as related to coworkers or managers. (1, 2)
2. Verbalize awareness of what triggers anger and how it is expressed. (1, 2, 3)
3. Verbally demonstrate an understanding of the rules of the workplace. (4)
4. Identify pain and hurt of past or current life that fuels anger. (5, 6)
5. Write a letter to target of anger that expresses anger and explains the hurts that cause the anger. (7)
6. Verbalize an understanding of the need for a process of forgiving others and self to reduce anger. (8, 9)
7. Write a letter of forgiveness to target of anger. (10)

THERAPEUTIC INTERVENTIONS

1. Explore current feelings of anger and the targets of and causes for anger as related to others within the workplace.
2. Confront/reflect angry behaviors in sessions.
3. Have employee read *Of Course You're Angry* (Rosellini and Worden) or *The Angry Book* (Rubin).
4. Attain verbal agreement/contract with employee to follow workplace rules regarding behavior to complete current probationary or warning period without further angry incidents.
5. Ask employee to list life experiences outside of work that have hurt and led to anger.
6. Empathize with and clarify employee's feelings of hurt

8. Describe incidents in which anger was expressed in poorly controlled terms and then state two alternative responses that would have been more constructive and less aggressive. (11, 12)

9. Cooperate with role-playing exercises to develop healthy coping techniques for angry feelings. (12)

10. Verbalize an understanding of the role that thoughts or beliefs play in precipitating feelings of hurt or anger. (13, 14)

11. Identify the self-talk about recent events that triggered anger. (13, 14, 15)

12. List the negative consequences that have occurred due to incidents of his/her expressions of uncontrolled anger. (16)

13. Attend assertiveness training classes to learn constructive ways to express feelings or opinions. (17)

14. Practice relaxation methods as a means of relieving tension and dissipating angry feelings. (18)

15. Verbalize feelings of anger in a controlled, assertive way. (12, 15, 17, 18, 19)

16. Report a decrease in the number and duration of angry outbursts. (12, 15, 17, 18, 19, 20)

and anger tied to past traumas.

7. Ask employee to write an angry letter to parents, spouse, manager, or whomever, focusing on the reasons for his/her anger toward that person. Process letter in session without sending it.

8. Discuss forgiveness of perpetrators of pain as a process of "letting go" of anger.

9. Suggest employee read *Forgive and Forget* (Smedes).

10. Ask employee to write a forgiving letter to the target of anger as a step toward letting go of anger. Process it in session.

11. Assign employee the task of describing two alternative, more constructive responses to a recent incident in which anger management was deficient and led to a negative outcome.

12. Using role-playing techniques, assist employee in developing non-self-defeating ways of handling angry feelings (e.g., speaking assertively not aggressively, using I messages, deep breathing, and time out).

13. Using a cognitive-behavioral framework, diagram with employee how intervening beliefs lead to emotional consequences following activating events.

—. _____
_____

—. _____
_____

—. _____
_____

14. Confront statements that reflect the concept of angry responses as occurring without intervening perceptions and beliefs.

15. Assist employee in identifying the self-talk, perceptions, or beliefs that trigger his/her feelings of anger at the target.

16. Ask employee to list three negative consequences of recent incidents of poor anger management.

17. Assign assertiveness training classes.

18. Demonstrate deep muscle relaxation or meditation techniques to facilitate self-calming.

19. Reinforce reports of conflict resolution and expression of anger in a calm, respectful, assertive manner.

20. Develop follow-up with employee to assess progress in goal-attainment and explore possible obstacles.

—. _____
_____

—. _____
_____

—. _____
_____

DIAGNOSTIC SUGGESTIONS

Axis I: 296.xx   Bipolar I Disorder
296.89   Bipolar II Disorder
312.8   Conduct Disorder
312.34   Intermittent Explosive Disorder
309.81   Posttraumatic Stress Disorder

_____   _____

_____   _____

Axis II: 301.7   Antisocial Personality Disorder
301.83   Borderline Personality Disorder
301.81   Narcissistic Personality Disorder
301.0   Paranoid Personality Disorder
301.9   Personality Disorder NOS

_____   _____

_____   _____

ANTISOCIAL BEHAVIOR

BEHAVIORAL DEFINITIONS

1. History of repeated disciplinary action (e.g., warnings, "write-ups") at work.
2. Pattern of interacting in an irritable, aggressive, and/or argumentative manner with supervisors.
3. History of attempts to manipulate or falsify workplace records such as the employment application, time cards, or attendance records.
4. Manipulation or abuse of corporate benefits such as vacation days, sick leave, disability, or workers' compensation.
5. Lack of respect for the property of others as demonstrated by stealing coworkers' or company property, plagiarizing coworkers' original creations, or intentionally damaging or sabotaging company equipment.
6. Failure to establish and maintain mutually cooperative relationships with coworkers as demonstrated by verbal and/or physical intimidation of coworkers, lying to or cheating coworkers, defaming the character of coworkers, or the sexual harassment and/or exploitation of coworkers.
7. Career history of frequent job changes.
8. Legal actions (e.g., court appearances, financial liens, warrants) that affect work attendance or work record keeping.
9. Reckless behavior in the workplace that endangers self or others.
10. Little or no remorse for rule breaking or hurting others.
11. Abuse of alcohol or other drugs.

__. _____
   _____
__. _____
   _____

—. _____
    _____

LONG-TERM GOALS

1. Become a responsible citizen of the workplace, adhering to work-place rules.
2. Become a reliable employee worthy of the trust of coworkers and managers.
3. Understand the impact of personal behavior on others.
4. Accept the appropriateness of consequences that follow behavioral choices.

—. _____
    _____

—. _____
    _____

—. _____
    _____

SHORT-TERM OBJECTIVES

1. Verbally demonstrate an understanding of the rules of the workplace. (1)
2. Consistently follow work-place rules; complete current probationary or warning period without further negative incidents. (1, 2)
3. Verbalize awareness of own tendency to be insensitive to feelings and rights of others. (3)
4. Verbally demonstrate and acknowledge the impact of personal behavior on

THERAPEUTIC INTERVENTIONS

1. Assign employee the homework of researching workplace policies, regulations, and disciplinary process by reading company literature or through meetings with human resources manager, union steward, or manager.
2. Reinforce employee's statements that demonstrate personal fallibility and/or responsibility for his/her behavioral choices.
3. Confront and limit employee's rude or argu-

the lives of coworkers.
(3, 4, 5, 6)

5. Decrease frequency of hostile or demeaning behavior. (3, 4, 5, 6)

6. Accept advice and feedback from EAP counselor without argument. (3, 6)

7. Identify the long-term consequences of being hurtful, uncaring, or totally self-centered. (7)

8. Apologize to coworker who has been hurt or whose rights have been trampled. (8)

9. Decrease statements blaming coworkers for workplace conditions. (2, 9)

10. Increase self-statements that acknowledge personal responsibility for behavioral choices. (2, 6, 9)

11. Increase incidents of helping behavior in the workplace (e.g., team work, group problem solving, task sharing). (6, 10)

12. List two prosocial methods to achieve a desired goal at work. (11)

13. Verbalize acceptance of the reality that others are needed to help attain his/her career goals. (12)

14. Actively seek out EAP counselor if uneasy or concerned about a lack of progress in any problem resolution. (13)

mentative behavior during the counseling session.

4. Reflect the employee's demeaning or hostile behavior.

5. Use self-disclosure to provide employee with examples of the reactions of others to his/her plans, verbalizations, or demeanor.

6. Use role-reversal techniques to provide employee with an awareness of the reactions of coworkers to his/her behavior.

7. Ask employee to logically list or diagram the longer-term consequences of self-centered, insensitive behavioral choices.

8. Have employee apologize to an injured or offended coworker or manager.

9. Confront blaming others for problems rather than accepting any personal responsibility for wrongdoing.

10. Assign as homework the "testing" of prosocial, kind, and helpful behavior in the workplace. Discuss reaction and outcome.

11. Ask employee to describe two prosocial plans or methods to achieve a desired goal in the workplace.

12. Assign employee the task of planning or mapping career goal(s). Actively challenge employee regarding the role

—. _____
   _____

—. _____
   _____

—. _____
   _____

that others will play in successfully attaining the goal.

13. Determine follow-up plan including specific dates with employee to ascertain progress and/or stumbling blocks to any problem resolution. Urge employee to not react with impulsivity and aggression.

—. _____
   _____
   _____

—. _____
   _____
   _____

—. _____
   _____

DIAGNOSTIC SUGGESTIONS

Axis I: 309.3   Adjustment Disorder With Disturbance
                           of Conduct
               303.90   Alcohol Dependence
               304.20   Cocaine Dependence
               312.34   Intermittent Explosive Disorder
               304.80   Polysubstance Dependence
               V71.01   Adult Antisocial Behavior

               _____   _____

               _____   _____

Axis II: 301.7   Antisocial Personality Disorder
               301.81   Narcissistic Personality Disorder
               301.0   Paranoid Personality Disorder

               _____   _____

               _____   _____

ANXIETY/PANIC

BEHAVIORAL DEFINITIONS

1. Excessive daily dread or worry that has no factual or logical basis and that interferes with job performance.
2. Symptoms of motor tension such as restlessness, tiredness, shakiness, or muscle tension.
3. Symptoms of autonomic hyperactivity such as palpitations, shortness of breath, dry mouth, trouble swallowing, nausea, or diarrhea.
4. Symptoms of hypervigilance such as feeling constantly on edge, concentration difficulties, trouble falling or staying asleep, and general state of irritability.
5. Periods of intense fear and/or physical discomfort characterized by sweating, trembling, heart pounding, perceived shortness of breath and/or choking, tightness in the chest, dizziness, fear of heart attack.
6. Difficulty staying at workstation due to a sense of impending, overwhelming anxiety.

__. _____
_____
__. _____
_____
__. _____
_____

LONG-TERM GOALS

1. Reduce overall level, frequency, and intensity of anxiety so that career development is not impaired.

2. Stabilize anxiety level while increasing general functioning, particularly job performance.
3. Terminate or manage panic symptoms such that confidence is restored and work is not interrupted.
4. Resolve the core conflict that is the source of the anxiety.

—. _____

_____

—. _____

_____

—. _____

_____

SHORT-TERM OBJECTIVES

1. Describe symptoms, their origination, and their precipitant. (1)
2. Verbalize an understanding of the role of distorted perceptions, cognition, and beliefs in causing anxiety symptoms. (2)
3. Identify the distorted perceptions, cognition, and beliefs that precipitate and maintain anxiety. (3, 4)
4. List positive, healthy, realistic cognitive self-talk messages that will be used to replace distorted cognition. (5, 6)
5. Report a decrease in the daily level of anxiety due to the use of behavioral coping mechanisms. (7, 8, 9, 10)
6. Implement appropriate relaxation and diversion activities, including the

THERAPEUTIC INTERVENTIONS

1. Explore employee's anxiety symptoms as to nature and stimulus events that may precipitate them.
2. Explain the role that perceptions and beliefs play in energizing and maintaining physiological overarousal.
3. Explore employee's distorted cognitive perceptions and beliefs that precipitate, exacerbate, and maintain anxiety response and retrain in adaptive cognition.
4. Assist employee in developing an awareness of the irrational nature of his/her fears.
5. Help employee develop reality-based cognitive messages that will increase self-confidence in coping with irrational fears.

focus on work itself, to decrease level of anxiety. (7, 8, 16)

7. Report the ability to manage panic symptoms through the use of cognitive and behavioral strategies. (5, 6, 8, 9)

8. Identify major life conflicts with particular emphasis on conflicts connected to the workplace or career situations. (11, 12, 13)

9. Verbalize insight into past conflicts and present anxiety. (12, 13)

10. Complete physician evaluation for medications. (14)

11. Take medications as described and report any side effects to appropriate professionals. (15)

12. Increase daily social and vocational involvement as demonstrated by the ability to remain at workstation and engage in productive work. (5, 7, 13, 16)

13. Agree to follow-up session to report on progress of anxiety control. (17)

—. _____

_____

—. _____

_____

—. _____

_____

6. Help employee develop healthy self-talk as a means of handling the anxiety.

7. Assist employee in developing coping strategies (e.g., increased social involvement, regular and relaxing work breaks, physical exercise) for his/her anxiety.

8. Explain and train employee in relaxation, focused breathing, meditation, or mindfulness. Provide homework assignment of regular practice.

9. Provide training exercise to demonstrate calming influence of a present focus.

10. Train employee in guided imagery for anxiety relief.

11. Ask employee to develop and process a list of key past and present life conflicts.

12. Assist employee in becoming aware of key unresolved life conflicts and in starting to work toward their resolution.

13. Reinforce employee's insights into past emotional issues and present anxiety.

14. Make a referral to a physician for a medication consultation.

15. Monitor medication compliance and effectiveness. Confer with physician.

16. Encourage and reinforce employee's increased social involvement as a means of

distraction from too much internal self-focus.

17. Develop follow-up plan and schedule follow-up visit with employee.

—. _____

_____

—. _____

_____

—. _____

_____

DIAGNOSTIC SUGGESTIONS

Axis I:	309.24	Adjustment Disorder With Anxiety
	300.00	Anxiety Disorder NOS
	300.02	Generalized Anxiety Disorder
	300.01	Panic Disorder without Agoraphobia
	300.21	Panic Disorder with Agoraphobia
	_____	_____
	_____	_____
Axis II:	301.82	Avoidant Personality Disorder
	_____	_____
	_____	_____

CHEMICAL DEPENDENCE

BEHAVIORAL DEFINITIONS

1. Consistent use of alcohol and/or other mood-altering drugs affecting previously satisfactory work performance.
2. Impaired functioning at work including substantial errors, delays in task completion, poor eye and hand coordination, and fragmented and incoherent speech.
3. Denial to coworkers and manager that chemical dependence is causing problems with functioning (e.g., "I only have a couple of drinks"; "I use only on weekends"; "It's their problem not mine") despite feedback that use of the substance is negatively affecting work performance as well as interpersonal relationships.
4. Continued drug and/or alcohol use despite experiencing persistent or recurring vocational problems that are directly caused by the use of the substance.
5. Suspension of important occupational activities because they interfere with the need to take drugs.
6. Continued use of mood-altering chemical after being told by manager that performance deterioration is increasing the probability of job termination.

—. _____
   _____

—. _____
   _____

—. _____
   _____

LONG-TERM GOALS

1. Accept chemical dependency as a problem and participate in a recovery program.
2. Accept alcohol abuse as a problem and participate in a "responsible drinking" program.
3. Establish a sustained recovery free from the use of all mood-altering substances.
4. Establish a sustained recovery through moderation management (controlled drinking) and the use of appropriate supports.
5. Acquire the necessary skills to maintain long-term sobriety from all mood-altering substances.
6. Establish a "drinkwise" individual moderation management (controlled drinking) program.

—. _____

   _____

—. _____

   _____

—. _____

   _____

SHORT-TERM OBJECTIVES

1. Identify the ways using drugs has negatively impacted work. (1, 2)

2. Cooperate with completing chemical dependence assessment instruments. (3)

3. Make verbal "I" statements that reflect acknowledgement and acceptance of chemical dependency. (4, 5)

4. Decrease the level of denial about using mood-altering substances as evidenced by more realistic, honest statements and the actual

THERAPEUTIC INTERVENTIONS

1. Gather a complete drug/alcohol history, including amount and pattern of use, signs and symptoms of use, and negative life consequences (social, legal, familial, vocational) resulting from employee's chemical dependency.

2. Ask employee to list the ways substance use has negatively impacted his/her life and discuss it with an EAP professional.

amount of use and its negative impact at work and in life in general. (2, 3, 5)

5. Verbalize increased knowledge of the problems associated with drinking and drugging and of the process of recovery. (5)

6. Identify the ways being sober could positively impact life at work and at home. (6)

7. Identify potential relapse triggers and develop strategies for constructively dealing with each trigger. (7)

8. State key changes necessary for the maintenance of sobriety in addition to simply not using. (8, 9)

9. Identify sources of ongoing support that will be used in maintaining sobriety. (10)

10. Comply with a physician's thorough physical exam. (11)

11. Verbalize an understanding of personality, social, and family factors that foster excessive drug use that negatively impacts functioning. (12, 13)

12. Verbalize how his/her living situation contributes to problems with drugs and acts as a hindrance to recovery. (14, 15)

13. State the need for a more stable, healthy living situation that will support recovery or responsible drinking. (14, 15, 16, 17)

3. Administer the Michigan Alcohol Screening Test (MAST), the Addiction Severity Index (ASI), or another alcohol screening tool to ensure that the diagnostic picture of substance abuse is accurate and reliable.

4. Assign employee the task of completing a First Step paper and then process it with either an AA group or sponsor, or EAP to receive feedback.

5. Suggest employee to read pamphlet on the disease concept of alcoholism as well as the concept of "moderate/risk reduction drinking" and select several key ideas to discuss.

6. Ask employee to make and process a list of the ways being sober could positively impact life at work and at home.

7. Assist employee in identifying the negative influence of people or situations that encourage relapse and ways to avoid them.

8. Plan with employee how to develop drug-free group friendships that will support sobriety.

9. Have employee meet with an NA or AA member who has been working with a 12-step program for several years and find out specifically how the program

14. Develop a written ongoing care plan that will support the maintenance of long-term sobriety. (10, 14, 18, 19)

15. Explore locations and times of AA meetings and other support mechanisms within the workplace to ensure relapse prevention. (10, 20)

16. Cooperate with follow-up arrangements developed in conjunction with the EAP to report on progress and/or difficulties during the coming year. (20, 21, 22)

—. _____

   _____

—. _____

   _____

—. _____

   _____

helped him/her stay sober; process the meeting with the employee.

10. Prepare employee for the Alcoholic Anonymous meeting.

11. Refer employee for thorough physical examinations to determine any physical effects of chemical dependence.

12. Investigate situational stress factors that may foster employee's chemical use.

13. Assess employee's intellectual, personality, and cognitive functioning as to his/her contribution to problems with drugs.

14. Evaluate the role of employee's living situation in fostering a pattern of chemical dependence.

15. Assign employee the task of listing negative influences for chemical dependence inherent in current living situation.

16. Encourage and assist employee in finding a more positive, stable living arrangement that will be supportive of recovery.

17. Assist employee in developing insight into life changes needed to maintain long-term sobriety.

18. Assign and review employee's written ongoing care plan to ensure it is adequate to maintain sobriety.

19. Develop an abstinence contract with employee regarding the use of his/her drug of choice. Process the emotional impact of this contract.

20. Direct employee to AA resources (e.g., meetings, contact people who have given permission to have their names released, reading material) within the workplace.

21. Follow up and support employee in his/her attempt to achieve and maintain abstinence or controlled drinking. Develop a regular pattern of meeting over the coming year.

22. After one-year review meeting, schedule and plan any additional follow-up as assessed to be necessary.

___. _____
_____

___. _____
_____

___. _____
_____

DIAGNOSTIC SUGGESTIONS

Axis I: 303.90   Alcohol Dependence
              305.00   Alcohol Abuse
              304.30   Cannabis Dependence
              305.20   Cannabis Abuse
              304.20   Cocaine Dependence
              304.60   Inhalant Dependence
              304.80   Polysubstance Dependence

              _____   _____

              _____   _____

Axis II: 301.7   Antisocial Personality Disorder

              _____   _____

              _____   _____

CHEMICAL DEPENDENCE—RELAPSE

BEHAVIORAL DEFINITIONS

1. Active use of mood-altering drugs, after a period of sobriety, either during work hours or within a few hours before or after work.
2. Reappearance, after a period of clean and sober living, of impaired functioning at work including errors, delays in task completion, poor eye and hand coordination, and fragmented speech.
3. Inability to stay free of mood-altering substances even though attending Alcoholics Anonymous (AA) meetings regularly.

___. _____
_____
___. _____
_____
___. _____
_____

LONG-TERM GOALS

1. Establish a lifestyle free of mood-altering drugs.
2. Comply with company substance abuse policy and substance abuse monitoring for the duration of employment.
3. Develop an understanding of personal relapse pattern to find more effective strategies to help sustain long-term recovery.
4. Develop an increased awareness of physical and mental relapse triggers that prompt the tendency to relapse.

___. _____
_____

—. _____

_____

_____

—. _____

_____

SHORT-TERM OBJECTIVES

1. Undergo comprehensive medical and psychiatric evaluations to rule out a medical, neurological, or biochemical problem that may be compromising recovery efforts or moderation management compliance. (1)

2. Verbalize the components of the recovery plan and acknowledge any aspects that were not being adhered to. (2)

3. Verbalize a level of motivation toward sobriety/recovery that will endure the rehabilitation/relapse prevention process. (3)

4. Identify the specific behaviors, attitudes, and feelings that led to the last relapse, focusing on triggers for the relapse. (4)

5. Identify behavior patterns that will need to be addressed in ongoing treatment and in support groups if sobriety is to be maintained. (4, 5, 6)

6. Recall all the relapses in the past years focusing on

THERAPEUTIC INTERVENTIONS

1. Motivate employee to have comprehensive medical and psychiatric evaluations to rule out medical problems that facilitate relapse.

2. Assess the employee's compliance to previously agreed to treatment plan, the current level of professional intervention and support, and his/her motivation to regain sobriety or a moderation management lifestyle.

3. If appropriate, challenge the employee's long-term commitment to recovery and reiterate the consequences of not following all aspects of the treatment plan.

4. Ask employee to develop a list of behaviors, attitudes, and feelings that could have triggered the relapse. Process the list in session.

5. Urge employee's completion of a relapse workbook (e.g., *The Staying Sober Workbook* by Gorski) and discussion of it with his/her therapist and AA sponsor.

patterns of similarities in stresses and feeling states. (5, 6, 7)

7. Provide release of information permission to EAP counselor for coordination of treatment with substance abuse counselor. (8)

8. Identify any changes in work situation that would support the recovery plan. (9, 10)

9. Confer with manager to develop strategies to ameliorate or combat coworkers' anger at employee's absence from workplace, which necessitated colleagues pick up the extra necessary work. (11)

10. Check in with EAP counselor at appointed times to review progress in recovery. (12, 13)

___. _____
_____

___. _____
_____

___. _____
_____

6. Suggest that employee work with his/her therapist to complete a relapse contract with a significant other/family member that identifies previous relapse-associated behaviors, attitudes, or emotions which will be stimuli for mutually determined warnings about relapse.

7. Assist employee in identifying patterns of similarities to relapse triggers over a number of efforts at recovery.

8. Develop an individualized follow-up plan.

9. With appropriate releases, check with treatment professional and employee's supervisor to see if employee is complying with treatment recommendations and if there are specific accommodations or a temporary change in work task which might support recovery at this time.

10. Provide short-term temporary insulation from potential high-stress situation at work by collaborating with employee's manager to alter working conditions (e.g., long hours and/or makeup work).

11. Encourage employee to talk to manager about ways to deal with coworker resentment over absenteeism.

12. Initiate the follow-up call and/or schedule an in-person appointment.

13. Meet with employee periodically (on a set schedule) to monitor follow-through with recovery plan and offer support.

___. _____

_____

___. _____

_____

___. _____

_____

DIAGNOSTIC SUGGESTIONS

Axis I:	303.90	Alcohol Dependence
	305.00	Alcohol Abuse
	304.30	Cannabis Dependence
	305.20	Cannabis Abuse
	304.20	Cocaine Dependence
	304.60	Inhalant Dependence
	304.80	Polysubstance Dependence
	_____	_____
	_____	_____
Axis II:	301.7	Antisocial Personality Disorder
	_____	_____
	_____	_____

COWORKER CONFLICT

BEHAVIORAL DEFINITIONS

1. Frequent or continual disagreements or arguments with a specific colleague.
2. Avoidance of eye contact when in the presence of the specific coworker.
3. Passive behavior and attitude in response to the specific colleague's questions, comments, and requests in meetings as well as in work/social situations.
4. Physical and/or verbal provocation of and use of aggressive language and gestures toward specific colleague.
5. Addresses the specific colleague disrespectfully both in content and in tone.
6. Initiation of discussions with other coworkers about a lack of respect for and refusal to work with the specific colleague.
7. Verbalization of dislike of coworker directly to him/her and other coworkers.
8. Angry and mean stares directed toward colleague which create a noticeable undercurrent of tension when colleague and employee are in a room together.
9. Persistent direct and indirect verbal interruptions when colleague is talking.
10. Inability to work on team projects with coworker.
11. Hypersensitivity to hints of critical comments by colleague.
12. Misinterpretation of benign events as having threatening personal significance.

—. _____

_____

—. _____

_____

—. _____
_____

LONG-TERM GOALS

1. Accept the need for tolerance of others within the workplace whom he/she may not like or whose lifestyles he/she may disapprove of.
2. When interacting with the specific coworker, focus on the context and goals of the meeting and how the colleague may be addressing the meeting's goals and agenda—not on the person him- or herself.
3. Recognize that holding and acting on personal grudges has no intrinsic or extrinsic value, particularly in the workplace.
4. Make a decision and commitment to improve communications at work and to strengthen relationships with coworkers by not contributing in any way to a negative work environment.
5. Before becoming upset with coworkers and their behaviors, try to understand what motivates them and why they are doing what they are doing.
6. Interact with the specific colleague without irrational anger or frustration.
7. Decrease the level of present conflict with the colleague while beginning to let go of past conflicts and fear/worries about him/her.
8. Stop blaming uninvolved coworkers for own personal and business disappointments and frustrations.
9. Report reduced vigilance and tension around specific colleague and more relaxed interaction with him/her as well.

—. _____
_____
_____

—. _____
_____

—. _____
_____

SHORT-TERM OBJECTIVES	THERAPEUTIC INTERVENTIONS
1. State the angry feelings toward the specific coworker and describe how	1. Explore employee's feelings of anger and how they are

those feelings are expressed verbally and behaviorally. (1)

2. Identify the objectionable qualities and behaviors of the specific colleague which lead to anger and frustration. (2, 3)

3. Verbalize the risks that aggressive and uncooperative behavior have on employment status, position within the company, and morale of coworkers. (4)

4. Verbalize an acceptance of own role in perpetuating interpersonal conflict. (5, 6)

5. Verbalize an awareness of the benefit of forgiveness of others at work and commit self to beginning the process of forgiveness. (6, 7, 8)

6. Use cognitive reframing to reduce or eliminate irrational anger or frustration. (9, 10)

7. Use biophysical relaxation and meditative mechanisms to reduce or eliminate irrational anger or frustration. (11)

8. State the behavioral alternatives that can be used when frustration or anger at a specific colleague builds. (11, 12)

9. Share the feelings associated with past emotionally painful situations that are recalled through contact with this specific colleague. (13, 14, 15)

expressed directly and indirectly.

2. Assist employee in identifying colleague's behaviors and qualities that anger and/or frustrate him/her.

3. Encourage employee to obtain a reality check of his/her beliefs regarding the specific colleague by discussing feelings and conclusions with others.

4. Discuss the negative consequences of uncooperative and overtly hostile behavior at work.

5. Confront employee when he/she blames others or fails to take responsibility for own actions, thoughts, and feelings.

6. Use role playing and role reversal to increase employee's empathy for others (e.g., the specific colleague) and understanding of the impact of his/her behavior on others.

7. Discuss forgiving others as a process of "letting go" of anger and frustration, which can reduce the risks of deteriorating emotional and physical health.

8. Encourage and reinforce employee in the practice of forgiveness as a means of healing internally and interpersonally.

9. Review employee's social interactions and explore distorted cognitive beliefs

10. Verbalize an acceptance of the insight that this specific colleague evokes feelings based on a relationship in his/her past. (15, 16, 17)

11. Decrease mean and angry stares directed toward specific colleague. (17, 18)

12. Increase eye contact with the specific colleague. (17, 18)

13. Write a letter of forgiveness to offending coworkers. (19)

—. _____
_____

—. _____
_____

—. _____
_____

operative during his/her interaction with others.

10. Help employee develop reality-based cognitive messages (e.g., I must be tolerant; I am only concerned with colleague's work performance; others forgive me so I must forgive others as well.) that will increase self-confidence in coping with irrational fears, anger, and frustration.

11. Train in coping strategies (diversion; deep, slow, rhythmic breathing; positive self-talk; muscle relaxation; etc.) to alleviate frustration and anger.

12. Use project management techniques that teach the employee how to focus on the business tasks at hand when working with the colleague.

13. Encourage employee to share feelings from past through active listening, unconditional positive regard, and gentle questioning.

14. Probe, discuss, and interpret possible symbolic meaning associated with the specific colleague and situation.

15. Reinforce employee's insights into a connection between past emotional pain and present frustration and anger.

16. Ask employee to make a connection between unresolved conflicts from the past and the feelings evoked by specific people (e.g., the disliked coworker) in the present.

17. Reinforce a reduction in anger caused by unrelated past pain that is expressed to coworkers in the present.

18. Review and verbally reinforce employee's reports of overcoming frustration and anger.

19. Ask employee to write a forgiving letter to the target of anger as a step toward letting go of the anger.

——. _____

_____

——. _____

_____

——. _____

_____

DIAGNOSTIC SUGGESTIONS

Axis I: 313.82   Identity Problem
309.4   Adjustment Disorder With Mixed Disturbance of Emotions and Conduct
V71.01   Adult Antisocial Behavior
_____   _____

_____

Axis II: 301.0   Paranoid Personality Disorder
301.22   Schizotypal Personality Disorder
_____   _____

_____   _____

CRITICAL INCIDENT

BEHAVIORAL DEFINITIONS

1. Experienced or witnessed a traumatic event which involved actual or threatened death, serious injury, or a threat to physical integrity.
2. Repeated flashbacks or persistent, unwanted memories of the traumatic event that make concentration difficult and heighten feelings of anxiety or depression.
3. Sleep difficulties and/or appetite disturbances following traumatic event.
4. Significant apprehension and/or fear of a repeat of the traumatic incident that make it difficult to carry out job responsibilities.
5. Feeling emotionally numb and having difficulty finding pleasure or happiness in usual life tasks, following the traumatic event.
6. Heightened irritability and anger, posttrauma.
7. Stress-related psychophysiological problems, such as low back pain, headaches, and gastrointestinal disorders, posttrauma.

—. _____
  _____
—. _____
  _____
  _____
—. _____
  _____

LONG-TERM GOALS

1. Integrate traumatic incident into his/her life story without massive repression or denial.
2. Recall traumatic event, when appropriate or necessary, without being overwhelmed by negative emotion.

3. Experience a full range of emotion, particularly finding happiness and pleasure in enjoyable activities.
4. Return to work schedule, activities, and locations associated with the traumatic event to carry out career and life tasks.

—. _____

_____

—. _____

_____

—. _____

_____

SHORT-TERM OBJECTIVES

1. Tell the complete story of the traumatic incident. (1)
2. Identify connection between his/her behavioral changes and the experience of the traumatic event. (2, 3)
3. Seek support from family members or friends to increase feelings of safety and security. (4, 5, 12)
4. Accept referral to a physician for a medication evaluation. (6)
5. Regain normal sleep and appetite patterns. (6, 7)
6. Verbalize an understanding that the emotional and psychophysiological reactions to the trauma are normal, expected, and not an indication of weakness or total loss of control. (8)
7. Identify and clarify the various emotions that are felt in reaction to the trauma. (9)

THERAPEUTIC INTERVENTIONS

1. Encourage employee to tell the complete story of the traumatic event, particularly soliciting his/her view of self, emotions, and thoughts during and immediately after the event.
2. Review the common psychological and behavioral responses to trauma as a means of preparing employee for changes he/she may experience.
3. Normalize employee's post-traumatic psychological and behavioral responses by explaining them in a context of common post-traumatic responses.
4. Encourage employee to tell his/her story to supportive family members and friends as a means of soliciting their support as opposed to shielding them from possi-

8. Verbalize a reduction in emotional numbness and report experiences of pleasure and happiness again. (10, 11)

9. Spend time with friends and/or family to increase a sense of security. (12)

10. List and implement any reasonable changes in daily routine that would increase the feeling of safety. (13)

11. Return to regular work schedule and nonwork activities with a manageable amount of anxiety. (6, 7, 13, 14, 15)

12. Identify negative self-talk that precipitates anxiety. (16, 22)

13. Replace negative self-talk with realistic, confident cognitions. (17, 22)

14. Report reduction in general level of anxiety. (7, 16, 17, 18, 23)

15. Report reduction in psychophysiological problems. (6, 7, 18, 22)

16. Report increased feelings of control over intrusive memories/flashbacks of the traumatic event. (19)

17. Display decreased level of irritability during the sessions. (20)

18. Terminate statements of revenge toward perpetrator of the traumatic event or revenge directed at the corporation (if traumatic event

ble worry, and as a means of desensitizing the memories of the traumatic event.

5. Review those with whom employee has shared his/her story.

6. Refer employee to a physician for a medication evaluation.

7. Teach employee relaxation and pleasant imagery as means of reducing tension and inducing sleep.

8. Ask employee to describe the emotional response of an "average person" experiencing the same traumatic event.

9. Challenge employee to use more emotion-based language (e.g., "I feel . . .") when describing the traumatic event or postevent functioning. Assist in clarifying the various emotions experienced.

10. Assign employee homework of spending time out with friends or family in an activity that employee admits he/she would usually find enjoyable.

11. Review employee's emotional reaction to homework assignment of having fun.

12. Suggest that employee accept offer from family or friend, or that employee request from a family member or friend, to spend time together after the traumatic event as a means of increas-

occurred at worksite). (21, 22, 23)

19. Attend a survivors self-help group. (23)

—. ————————————————
————————————————

—. ————————————————
————————————————

—. ————————————————
————————————————

ing perceptions of safety and security.

13. Problem-solve with employee any changes he/she could make in daily routine that would increase perception of safety.

14. Encourage and reinforce employee's return to work and/or daily routine.

15. Follow up and process employee's emotional reaction to returning to the place of the traumatic event and/or leaving loved ones for the workday.

16. Explore employee cognitions that predict doom or reflect an inability to cope, and demonstrate how those cognitions maintain disabling anxiety.

17. Encourage employee to replace irrational, negative-prediction cognition with affirming and reasonable self-statements.

18. Encourage and explain anxiety-reducing value of here-and-now living.

19. Demonstrate thought-stopping technique for employee.

20. Provide feedback to employee regarding the general level of anger he/she is expressing in verbalizations and body language. Reinforce a more relaxed, less agitated demeanor.

21. Encourage employee to redirect anger regarding traumatic incident and/or its perpetrator into appropriate channels of redress (e.g., court system, volunteer activities, survivors' action groups, corporate safety task forces).

22. Connect unfocused or irrational thoughts of revenge to continued levels of tension and psychophysiological distress.

23. Refer employee to a self-help group for survivors of similar traumatic events.

—. _____
   _____
—. _____
   _____
—. _____
   _____

DIAGNOSTIC SUGGESTIONS

Axis I: 309.81   Posttraumatic Stress Disorder
              309.28   Adjustment Disorder With Mixed Anxiety and
                        Depressed Mood
              312.34   Intermittent Explosive Disorder
              308.3   Acute Stress Disorder
              _____   _____

Axis II: 301.9   Personality Disorder NOS
              _____   _____
              _____   _____

DEPRESSION

BEHAVIORAL DEFINITIONS

1. Frequently verbalizes statements that are critical of coworkers, management, work conditions, supervisors, and/or pay rate.
2. Displays extreme passivity and compliance with direction given by others.
3. Does not fulfill duties and expectations of team membership.
4. Shows a lack of initiative in resolving work-related problems.
5. Productivity is below expected levels.
6. Number of errors made is above expected levels.
7. Displays flat or depressed affect.
8. Absenteeism rate is above acceptable standards.
9. Acknowledges use of drugs and/or alcohol to cope with depressive feelings.
10. Lack of energy reflected in a low activity level, complaints of tiredness, and/or tardiness.
11. Social withdrawal evident in relationships with coworkers
12. Ignores safety regulations in the work environment through poor concentration and lack of attention to details.

—. _____

_____

_____

—. _____

_____

_____

—. _____

_____

LONG-TERM GOALS

1. Alleviate depressed mood and return to previous levels of effective functioning in the work setting.
2. Recognize depression as the cause of critical, dissatisfied attitude, below average work performance, or low energy, and seek appropriate treatment to resolve mood disorder.
3. Terminate the abuse of alcohol and/or illicit drugs as a coping mechanism and accept a referral for treatment for depression.
4. Develop the ability to recognize situations and thoughts that trigger and usually lead to depressive states.

—. _____

_____

—. _____

_____

—. _____

_____

SHORT-TERM OBJECTIVES

1. Verbalize an acceptance that depression is the cause of poor work performance. (1, 2)

2. Identify the symptoms of depression that are revealed in the work setting. (2)

3. Verbally identify the source of depressed mood. (3, 4)

4. Verbalize a belief in personal control over feelings and that there is a difference between recognizing an emotion and being controlled by it. (4, 5)

5. Identify personal signs of stress overload. (6)

THERAPEUTIC INTERVENTIONS

1. Teach employee how depression can lead to reduced motivation to perform, loss of interest, low energy, loss of confidence, and social withdrawal in the work setting.

2. Explore the signs and symptoms of depression that employee experiences in the employment situation.

3. Help employee identify the causes within past or present work or home environment for his/her depressed mood.

4. Help employee explore and label his/her feelings.

6. State the behavioral alternatives that will be used when stress levels build and fear develops over becoming depressed or overwhelmed. (7)

7. Express to therapist feelings of anger, helplessness, or frustration toward coworkers or supervisor. (8)

8. Attend a self-help group that allows free exploration and expression of honest feelings and gives objective feedback. (9)

9. Identify unrealistic wishes that the company fulfill personal needs beyond the scope of an employer's responsibility and state a plan to meet those needs in a more realistic way. (10)

10. Verbalize an awareness of the relationship between repressed anger and depressed mood. (11)

11. Develop and commit to an activity plan that includes regular exercise, recreational activities, a routine sleep pattern, and a balanced diet. (12)

12. Verbalize an understanding that living in the past can trigger feelings of guilt and regret, while living in the future can create undue worry. (13, 14)

13. List ways to reorient life toward living in the present rather than the past or future. (13, 14)

5. Teach employee that his/her behavior can be controlled by positive thoughts rather than negative feelings.

6. Teach employee the signs and symptoms of stress overload (e.g., decreased energy, shallow breathing, heart rate increase, sweating, weakness, fear of loss of control over emotions or behavior) and help identify those that he/she experiences.

7. Develop a list of behavioral alternatives that are acceptable in the work setting to deal with work stress (e.g., talk to supervisor, take a brief break away from stress-producing situation, use deep-breathing exercises to relax, imagine a pleasant scene that induces serenity).

8. Probe employee's feelings of rage or helplessness related to personnel at work.

9. Have employee attend a self-help group that encourages free expression of feelings and gives constructive, objective feedback.

10. Explore any unrealistic needs that employee expects his/her employment situation to satisfy (e.g., substitute for lack of family closeness, too frequent praise or recognition, social life substitute) and develop realistic plans to meet those

14. Identify those toward whom grudges are held in the work or home setting and the causes for the anger or resentment. (15, 16)

15. Verbalize an understanding of the need for and benefits of forgiveness of self and others at home or work. (15, 16)

16. Identify successful, constructive experiences that occurred in the work setting as a means of building a reservoir of positive memories that can lead to pleasant feelings toward employment. (17)

17. Express positive feelings toward work responsibilities, coworkers, and supervisors. (17, 18)

18. Increase rate of productivity within the work setting. (19, 20)

19. Reduce frequency of absenteeism and tardiness. (20)

20. Demonstrate through clean random urine samples that drugs and alcohol are no longer being used as a means of coping with negative feelings. (21, 22)

21. Meet with a physician for an evaluation of physical health and the need for psychotropic medications. (23, 24)

22. Take prescribed medications responsibly at the times ordered by the physician. (24)

needs outside of the work setting.

11. Teach employee about the relationship between unexpressed feelings and depression.

12. Teach employee the emotional and physical benefits of a consistent routine to his/her life and assign a plan to institute regular exercise, sleep, recreation, and nutritional meals.

13. Discuss how living in the past can lead to guilt and living in the future can lead to unproductive anxiety.

14. Assign employee the task of listing ways that his/her life can be reoriented to the present (e.g., list tasks to be accomplished today and cross off each one as it is completed, take time each day to do something pleasurable, talk to coworkers about how they are feeling today).

15. Assist employee in identifying those with whom he/she is angry at home or work and discuss the relationship between unexpressed anger and depression.

16. Discuss the forgiveness of others as a process of letting go of anger that can be destructive to emotional and physical health as well as reduce productivity in the workplace through loss

23. Identify cognitive self-talk regarding work or other aspects of life that is engaged in to support depression. (25, 26)

24. Replace negative and self-defeating messages about home or work with verbalization of positive, realistic messages. (25, 26)

25. Comply with all psychotherapeutic recommendations and interventions. (27)

__. _____

   _____

__. _____

   _____

__. _____

   _____

of concentration, energy, and focus.

17. Assist employee in developing a list of positive experiences that have occurred in the workplace.

18. Reinforce the expression of positive feelings regarding any and all aspects of the employment setting

19. Monitor, encourage, and reinforce any increase in productivity.

20. Develop a list of legitimate reasons for absenteeism or tardiness and then reinforce employee for reducing absenteeism and tardiness.

21. Confront employee's substance abuse as a means of coping with negative emotions and evaluate the severity of any addictions.

22. Monitor employee for freedom from substance abuse by using random urine tests and refer him/her for substance abuse evaluation and treatment as necessary.

23. Refer employee to a physician for a medical exam and evaluation of the need for psychotropic intervention.

24. Monitor and reinforce employee for consistent cooperation with medication treatment.

25. Assist employee in developing an awareness of cognitive messages that reinforce hopelessness, helplessness, and depression.

26. Help employee identify positive cognitive messages that will mediate elevation of mood and attitude.

27. Develop with employee a long-term treatment plan that will sustain the present gains in mood stability and increased work performance and satisfaction.

__. _____
   _____

__. _____
   _____

__. _____
   _____

DIAGNOSTIC SUGGESTIONS

Axis I	309.0	Adjustment Disorder With Depressed Mood
	296.xx	Bipolar I Disorder
	296.89	Bipolar II Disorder
	300.4	Dysthymic Disorder
	296.xx	Major Depressive Disorder
	_____	_____
	_____	_____

DISCIPLINARY STRESS

BEHAVIORAL DEFINITIONS

1. Feelings of depression, anxiety, anger, and low self-esteem associated with discipline process.
2. Sleep and appetite difficulties related to current disciplinary stress.
3. Productivity loss stemming from fear and doubt about job security.
4. Unusually short-tempered and angry with manager, coworkers, and company.
5. Worry and fear about disclosing situation to spouse and family.
6. Concerns about potential loss of income and status.
7. Uncertainty and frustration about the solution to situation.
8. Confusion about the progressive disciplinary process used by employer.

—. _____
   _____
—. _____
   _____
—. _____
   _____

LONG-TERM GOALS

1. Change work behaviors to eliminate further disciplinary action.
2. Find new position either in or outside company based on accurate self-perception of competencies and desires.
3. Develop more awareness of critical factors that determine success at specific job and specific company.
4. Develop a balanced outlook on work, identity, and life outside of work.

5. Establish positive open communication with manager and ask for constructive feedback on a regular basis to prevent poor performance evaluation.
6. Actively try to anticipate manager's needs.
7. Whenever possible, try to engage in work activities that will reflect well on manager.

—. _____
   _____
   _____

—. _____
   _____
   _____

—. _____
   _____

SHORT-TERM OBJECTIVES

1. Verbalize a clear and concrete understanding of current performance deficiencies or behavior aberrations. (1, 2)

2. List self-perceptions of performance deficiencies and compare them to the manager's documented disciplinary report. (1, 2)

3. Describe work history including any previous work-related disciplinary problems. (3, 4)

4. Verbalize the pattern of work-related disciplinary problems stemming from similar behavior. (3, 4, 5)

5. Research and report an understanding of the workplace progressive disciplinary process as it affects self at this time and actions

THERAPEUTIC INTERVENTIONS

1. Actively encourage employee to tell his/her story about the current disciplinary problems.

2. Actively listen to employee, empathize with situation as appropriate, and ask questions that aim to clarify the employee's perception of his/her behavior as compared to the disciplinary report.

3. Explore whether employee has experienced previous disciplinary problems at work.

4. Gather a complete work history, including current and past successes, frustrations, and challenges.

5. Draw parallels between current situation and difficulties in the past.

taken to resolve the problem. (6)

6. Obtain from supervisor reports of technical performance of work responsibilities and adequate behaviors. (7)

7. Verbalize agreement to share information regarding the disciplinary actions with key social support people. (8, 9)

8. Verbalize what expectations are held for emotional or social need satisfaction within the work setting. (10)

9. State a plan to expand social and recreational interests outside of work. (11)

10. Seek out and attend training seminars that will increase level of necessary job skills. (12)

11. Eliminate projection of blame for work difficulties and admit responsibility for the current situation. (13)

12. Report feeling less anger and give examples of redirecting those feelings evoked by the disciplinary process. (14)

13. Report the development of a more positive relationship with manager. (15, 16, 17)

14. Practice deep muscle relaxation technique to reduce tension. (18)

15. Actively use relaxation, recreational diversion, and assertiveness to redirect

6. Elicit from employee the steps of the disciplinary process that have occurred and what she/he has done to resolve the issue.

7. Assess the current problem and determine root cause, be it technical competency, interpersonal conflict with manager or coworker, quantity of work, substance abuse, etc.

8. Assess the duration and strength of employee's relationship with spouse/significant other to determine whether to encourage discussion of the disciplinary situation before resolution.

9. Assess the need to intervene and discuss the situation with the employee's manager or human resource representative if there is a need for employee advocacy.

10. Explore any unrealistic needs for which the employee is seeking satisfaction in the workplace (e.g., substitute for lack of family, closeness, excessive praise or recognition, social-life substitute).

11. Assist employee in developing realistic plans to meet emotional and social needs outside of the workplace.

12. Review availability of training opportunities, both inside and outside the company, that may address technical job deficiencies.

anxious and troubling feelings about the current experience. (14, 15, 18)

16. Regain usual sleep and appetite/eating patterns. (8, 9, 11, 16, 18)

17. Improve punctuality and attendance. (13, 19)

18. Inform EAP of progress being made on disciplinary problem. (20)

—. _____
    _____

—. _____
    _____

—. _____
    _____

13. Reframe destructive blaming and damming cognition/statements to assist employee in taking responsibility for his/her own behavior.

14. Encourage employee to dissipate anger and anxiety through exercise, social distraction, and recreational diversion.

15. Suggest employee read books to enhance active communication such as *No-Nonsense Communication,* by Kirkpatrick, or *Are You Listening,* by Nichols and Stevens.

16. Model and role-play assertive communication to improve relationships with managers.

17. Have employee read assertiveness training books such as *Your Perfect Right,* by Alberti and Emmons.

18. Demonstrate self-relaxation techniques.

19. Monitor employee's punctuality and attendance, encouraging personal responsibility and assessing for possible substance abuse problem.

20. Follow up with employee to determine whether disciplinary problem is progressively being resolved and if additional support is needed.

—. _____
   _____

—. _____
   _____

—. _____
   _____

DIAGNOSTIC SUGGESTIONS

Axis I: 309.0   Adjustment Disorder With Depressed Mood
            309.24   Adjustment Disorder With Anxiety
            309.28   Adjustment Disorder With Mixed Anxiety and
                      Depressed Mood
            V62.2   Occupational Problem
            _____   _____
            _____   _____

EATING DISORDER

BEHAVIORAL DEFINITIONS

1. Consistent verbal comments about body image that relate an unrealistic assessment of being too fat or a strong denial of being emaciated.
2. Frequent expressions of irrational worry and fear about becoming overweight, which coworkers find distressing.
3. Chronic, rapid consumption of large quantities of high-carbohydrate food.
4. Extreme weight loss (and amenorrhea in females) with refusal to maintain a minimal healthy weight.
5. Very limited ingestion of food and high frequency of secret self-induced vomiting, inappropriate use of laxatives, and/or excessive strenuous exercises.
6. Frequent use of the bathroom after eating for periods which last over ten minutes and leave evidence of vomiting.
7. Constant presence of food on employee's desk or in work area.
8. Continual snacking throughout the workday.
9. Refusal to join colleagues for lunch or, if he/she does accompany others, only picking at a very light meal, not eating normally.
10. Lack of energy and ability to concentrate due to minimal amount of food intake.

___. _____
_____

___. _____
_____
_____

___. _____
_____

LONG-TERM GOALS

1. Commit to treatment to restore normal eating patterns, body weight, balanced fluid and electrolyte levels, and a realistic perception of body size.
2. Cease pattern of binge eating and vomiting with a return to normal eating of enough nutritious foods to maintain healthy weight.
3. Find support and comfort in ongoing resources (e.g., Overeater Anonymous) that will assist in maintaining healthy eating patterns.
4. Through treatment and support, learn to separate food from feelings and develop a sense of peace in relation to food and eating.

—. _____

_____

—. _____

_____

—. _____

_____

SHORT-TERM OBJECTIVES

1. Give accurate and emotionally honest history of eating disorder. (1, 2)

2. List and discuss previous attempts to resolve problem. (3)

3. Admit to a lack of control over the eating disorder and a need for professional help. (4, 5, 7)

4. Articulate fears and ambivalence about getting professional help to solve problem. (5, 7)

5. Verbalize feelings of low self-esteem related to eating disorder. (6)

THERAPEUTIC INTERVENTIONS

1. Establish trusting relationship with employee and explain EAP role in helping him/her find appropriate assistance to solve problem and the follow-up activity which will last until the problem is solved.

2. Gather a comprehensive history of employee's eating problem.

3. Review employee's unsuccessful attempts to control the eating problem.

4. Confront any denial of the seriousness of the problem.

6. Sign release of information forms for physician, dentist, and mental health professional. (7, 8)

7. Cooperate with a comprehensive physical examination. (7, 9)

8. Cooperate with a dental examination. (7, 10)

9. Cooperate with a comprehensive evaluation by a mental health professional. (7, 11)

10. Honestly acknowledge and articulate reactions to medical, psychological, and dental examinations. (12)

11. Comply with treatment recommendations. (13, 14)

12. List and articulate resistance to and hesitations about following treatment recommendations. (15)

13. Show evidence of appropriate eating, weight gain, and positive self-image. (16)

__. _____
    _____
__. _____
    _____
__. _____
    _____

5. Recommend and reinforce seeking the help of a mental health professional.

6. Explore employee's feelings of a negative self-image.

7. Discuss the importance of a comprehensive medical, psychiatric, and dental evaluation to determine the severity of the problem.

8. Obtain a release of information from employee so that the EAP can share relevant information with physician, dentist, and mental health professional(s).

9. Refer the employee to a physician for a comprehensive medical examination.

10. Refer the employee to a dentist for a dental exam.

11. Refer the employee to a mental health professional for a comprehensive evaluation and a treatment plan recommendation.

12. Follow up with the employee after each evaluation to see how it went and ensure that therapeutic recommendations are considered.

13. Facilitate communication between the medical professionals to maximize understanding of the problem and develop a comprehensive, coordinated treatment plan.

14. Follow up and encourage employee to engage in recommended treatment by health care professionals.

15. Meet with employee periodically to reduce any resistance to continuing treatment.

16. Reinforce all evidence of progress in establishing normal eating patterns and positive self-evaluation.

___. _____
_____
___. _____
_____
___. _____
_____

DIAGNOSTIC SUGGESTIONS

Axis I: 307.50   Eating Disorder NOS
307.1   Anorexia Nervosa
307.51   Bulimia Nervosa
_____   _____

Axis II: 301.4   Obsessive-Compulsive Personality Disorder
_____   _____
_____   _____

EDUCATIONAL DEFICITS

BEHAVIORAL DEFINITIONS

1. Lacks necessary credit requirements for high school diploma.
2. Failure to take classes or attempt to pass GED test.
3. Lack of necessary reading and writing skills to complete required reports for his/her employment position.
4. Functional illiteracy which limits any promotional activity.
5. Employment termination due to a lack of necessary math, writing, and/or reasoning skills.
6. No marketable job skills.

—. _____
   _____
—. _____
   _____
—. _____
   _____

LONG-TERM GOALS

1. Seek out vocational training to obtain marketable employment skills.
2. Enroll in and complete literacy training program.
3. Recognize the need for high school completion or GED and enroll in necessary courses to attain diploma or pass GED test.
4. Commit to ongoing study with an accredited institution of learning.
5. Termination of denial and open acknowledgement of reading, math, or job skill deficiencies.

—. _____
_____
_____

—. _____
_____
_____

—. _____
_____

SHORT-TERM OBJECTIVES

1. Identify, articulate, and list aspirations and goals in relation to literacy and/or other educational deficiencies. (1)

2. Identify and list the specific stumbling blocks that have prevented him/her from becoming literate. (2)

3. Share feelings of shame or embarrassment that have been associated with lack of reading ability or job skill. (2, 3, 6)

4. List the negative effects of illiteracy and/or lack of job skill training. (4)

5. List the potential positive consequences of increasing reading ability and/or job skill training. (5)

6. Verbally acknowledge the need for further education in basic reading and writing skills, or job skill training. (4, 5, 6)

7. Make the necessary contacts to enroll in an appropriate educational program. (7, 8, 9)

THERAPEUTIC INTERVENTIONS

1. Explore the current nature and severity of employee's educational deficiencies.

2. Assist employee in identifying his/her reasons for resistance to education or the role denial has played in failure to correct educational deficiencies.

3. Facilitate employee openness regarding frustration, shame, or embarrassment surrounding lack of reading ability, educational achievement, or vocational skill.

4. Assist employee in identifying the negative effects on his/her life that have resulted from functional illiteracy or no job skills.

5. Assist employee in identifying the potential positive outcomes of further education.

6. Assess employee's intelligence, aptitude, and motivation to address deficiencies. Reinforce a commitment to obtaining further education and/or skill training.

8. Make an appointment and attend interview for admission to skill training or school. (7, 8, 9)

9. Attend classes to obtain further vocational or literacy training. (10)

10. Apply for GED. (11)

11. Take GED examinations. (11, 12)

12. Review progress in education and/or job skill training program. (13)

13. List the goals and objectives of future educational activities based on workplace needs and future aspirations. (14)

14. Review goals/objectives and develop a plan for goal achievement. (15)

___. _____
   _____

___. _____
   _____

___. _____
   _____

7. Direct employee toward community or corporate resources for obtaining further academic or job skill training.

8. Assign employee the task of making preliminary contact with vocational and/or educational training agencies and report back the experience of the contact.

9. Contact a community resource to understand what the enrollment process consists of. Pass this information on to employee to facilitate his/her follow-through and reduce anxiety.

10. Monitor and support employee's attendance at educational or vocational classes.

11. Supply employee with information on community education resources for GED testing.

12. Monitor and encourage follow-through with taking GED examination.

13. Assess employee's progress in the educational program.

14. Assist employee in identifying further educational needs that would improve level of challenge at work and chances for advancement.

15. Develop a plan with employee for meeting educational goals.

—. _____
    _____
—. _____
    _____
—. _____
    _____

DIAGNOSTIC SUGGESTIONS

Axis I: 315.2   Disorder of Written Expression
              315.00   Reading Disorder
              V62.2   Occupational Problem
              V62.3   Academic Problem
              _____   _____

Axis II: 317   Mild Mental Retardation
              V62.89   Borderline Intellectual Functioning
              _____   _____
              _____   _____

FINANCIAL STRESS

BEHAVIORAL DEFINITIONS

1. Fear of losing housing because of an inability to meet monthly mortgage payment.
2. Creditors are suing to garnish wages.
3. Credit card bills (of employee, spouse, or child) far exceed the family's ability to pay them.
4. Credit union has alerted employee that he/she has reached the maximum in terms of loans.
5. Defaulted more than once on monthly loan payments.
6. Overdrawn on checking account due to a lack of adequate reserves.

—. _____
   _____
—. _____
   _____
—. _____
   _____

LONG-TERM GOALS

1. Establish the ability to meet current financial obligations through an increase in income and/or a reduction in expenses.
2. Establish and maintain a balanced budgetary plan for future income and expenditures.
3. Strictly follow a plan of debt repayment and budgeted living developed with Consumer Credit Counseling.
4. Actively master the temptation to buy more by redirecting thoughts to the consequences of such behavior.

___. _____
    _____
___. _____
    _____
___. _____
    _____

SHORT-TERM OBJECTIVES

1. Admit to having financial problems. (1, 2)
2. Write a complete list of financial obligations including mortgage or rent, utility bills, credit card payments, car loans, insurance premiums, household expenses, etc. (3)
3. Develop a realistic plan to solve the financial crisis. (4)
4. List the obstacles that have stood in the way of mastering these financial problems and the stress that ensues. (5)
5. Openly acknowledge any chemical dependence problems that may exist for anyone within the home. (6, 7)
6. Accept a referral to a mental health professional for a comprehensive chemical dependence evaluation. (8)
7. Comply with treatment recommendations of a mental health professional. (9)
8. Attend Credit Counseling initial evaluation and

THERAPEUTIC INTERVENTIONS

1. Provide a supportive, comforting environment by being empathic, warm, and sensitive to the fact that the topic may illicit guilt, shame, and embarrassment from the employee.
2. Ask employee probing questions to ascertain a complete history of his/her financial difficulties and the stress that they engender.
3. Assist employee in compiling a complete list of financial obligations.
4. Encourage employee to face problems to be able to gain control over the situation.
5. Review employee's previous attempts to address the financial obligations.
6. Probe for excessive alcohol or other drug use by the employee by asking questions from the CAGE or MAST (Michigan Alcohol Screening Test) screening instruments for substance abuse.

develop a plan for fiscal management. (10)

9. Attend Credit Counseling follow-up sessions and cooperate with the plan for debt retirement. (11)

10. Keep weekly and monthly records of financial income and expenses. (12)

11. Report each instance of a debt resolution as it occurs. (13)

12. Use cognitive review strategies to control the impulse to make unnecessary and unaffordable purchases. (14, 15)

—. _____
   _____

—. _____
   _____

—. _____
   _____

7. Explore the possibility of alcohol or drug use by family member or significant other.

8. Refer employee to a mental health professional for comprehensive assessment relating to substance abuse or psychiatric disorder.

9. Encourage employee to collaborate and comply with mental health/substance abuse treatment plan.

10. Refer employee to a nonprofit, no-cost credit counseling service to develop a budgetary plan of debt repayment.

11. Encourage employee attendance at all credit counseling sessions and self-discipline to control spending within budgetary guidelines.

12. Encourage employee to keep weekly and monthly records of income and outflow. Review records weekly and reinforce responsible financial behavior.

13. Offer praise and ongoing encouragement of debt resolution.

14. Teach employee the cognitive strategy of asking self before each purchase: Is this purchase absolutely necessary? Can we afford this? Do we have the cash to pay for this without incurring any further debt?

15. Urge employee to avoid all impulse buying by delaying every purchase until 24 hours of thought and buying only from a prewritten list of items.

___. _____

      _____

___. _____

      _____

___. _____

      _____

DIAGNOSTIC SUGGESTIONS

Axis I:

309.24	Adjustment Disorder With Anxiety
309.0	Adjustment Disorder With Depressed Mood
309.28	Adjustment Disorder With Mixed Anxiety and Depressed Mood
303.90	Alcohol Dependence
305.00	Alcohol Abuse
304.30	Cannabis Dependence
296.0x	Bipolar I Disorder, Single Manic Episode
V62.2	Occupational Problem
V61.1	Partner Relational Problem
_____	_____
_____	_____

Axis II:

301.7	Antisocial Personality Disorder
301.81	Narcissistic Personality Disorder
_____	_____
_____	_____

GAMBLING

BEHAVIORAL DEFINITIONS

1. Preoccupation with gambling activities interferes with financial, work, social, and family responsibilities.
2. Excessive indebtedness due to gambling activity causes a significant hardship.
3. Repeated promises to terminate or control gambling have been broken.
4. Denies ever borrowing money from colleagues even though it has occurred repeatedly.
5. Complains about debts and requests family members to help repay them.
6. Organizes gambling junkets such as trips to popular casinos.
7. Gambling-related charges incurred on corporate credit card that are not approved and/or submitted for reimbursement.
8. Borrowing money from colleagues which is never paid back.
9. Continually organizes office paycheck or sports pools.

__. _____
   _____
   _____
__. _____
   _____
__. _____
   _____

LONG-TERM GOALS

1. Stop all gambling activity and take responsibility for indebtedness and family financial planning.
2. Accept gambling as a problem and participate in a recovery program to minimize the recurrence of the problem.
3. Develop sound financial planning for self that strictly budgets for family expenses before any discretionary spending.
4. Actively participate in prevention services to minimize the risk of a relapse into gambling.

—. _____

_____

—. _____

_____

—. _____

_____

SHORT-TERM OBJECTIVES

1. Describe the history of the development of problems with gambling and the current extent to which gambling dominates his/her life. (1, 2)
2. Verbalize awareness and acceptance of the fact that gambling is interfering with major aspects of life. (1, 2, 3)
3. Describe the exciting feeling that is generated by the gambling behavior and the unsuccessful attempts at controlling the behavior that generates that feeling. (2, 4)

THERAPEUTIC INTERVENTIONS

1. Actively listen to employee's concerns and ask questions that will facilitate greater understanding of the gambling pattern.
2. Gather a history of the problem and of previous attempts to control his/her gambling.
3. Explore the effects the problem has had on work and family.
4. Expose the rush that is felt by the uncertainty of the wager.
5. Help employee uncover the fear that surrounds having to give up the excitement of gambling.

4. Verbally acknowledge the fears that stand in the way of the ability to quit gambling. (2, 4, 5, 6)

5. List specifically the ways gambling has adversely affected his/her life. (3, 7)

6. Make a commitment to seek help from a treatment professional with the hope of terminating gambling. (5, 7, 8, 19)

7. Verbalize an understanding and acceptance of the need for total commitment to change. (9, 10, 11)

8. Make an appointment with a mental health professional with a specialization in gambling to evaluate the type of treatment needed. (12, 13, 14)

9. Cooperate with a comprehensive psychiatric evaluation to rule out any medical, neurological, or biochemical problems that are compounding or aggravating the addictive behavior. (12, 13, 14)

10. Agree to regular follow-up meetings with EAP. (14)

11. Report on treatment progress to EAP. (15, 16, 17, 18)

12. Terminate all gambling behavior at workplace and report no other gambling elsewhere. (17, 19)

6. Explore family/significant other dynamics using a systems theory approach to gain a greater understanding of the gambling problem.

7. Assist employee in listing specific negative consequences on his/her life that result from gambling.

8. Assess employee's motivation to seek assistance to resolve problem and then refer him/her to a mental health professional.

9. Discuss with employee the process of change and the need for a total commitment to the process.

10. Discuss with employee the process of treatment, including the substitution of alternatives for problem behaviors such as relaxation, desensitization, assertion, and positive self-talk.

11. Talk with employee about specific alternative behaviors that may include restructuring his/her environment (e.g., avoiding or removing self from high-risk people and locations that have prompted gambling in the past).

12. Refer employee to a mental health professional with a specialization in gambling, knowing that employee's

—. _____
   _____

—. _____
   _____

—. _____
   _____

gambling problems may be a variant of an obsessive-compulsive disorder.

13. Ask employee to sign release of information forms to share appropriate information with mental health professionals.

14. Determine with employee how and when EAP follow-up should take place to determine if and how progress is being made to reach treatment goals and problem resolution.

15. Confront any noted resistance to following the mental health professional's treatment plan.

16. Follow up with employee and referring professionals to ensure that he/she kept appointment and to coordinate and encourage compliance to treatment plan.

17. Reinforce employee's attempts to terminate gambling.

18. Contact treatment professional to determine if and how employee is progressing in reaching treatment goals and to collaboratively determine if the EAP can assist the process with a workplace accommodation.

19. Refer employee to a Gamblers Anonymous group as an adjunct to his/her recovery program.

___. _____
      _____
___. _____
      _____
___. _____
      _____

DIAGNOSTIC SUGGESTIONS

Axis I: 312.31   Pathological Gambling
                309.3   Adjustment Disorder With Disturbance of
                           Conduct

                _____   _____
                _____   _____

Axis II: 301.4   Obsessive-Compulsive Personality Disorder
                301.7   Antisocial Personality Disorder

                _____   _____
                _____   _____

GRIEF AND LOSS

BEHAVIORAL DEFINITIONS

1. Suffered the death of a significant person in his/her life.
2. Experienced losses (e.g., job, friend moving away, child leaving home, injury, or poor health) that have substantially altered his/her life.
3. Complains of a constant ache that does not go away.
4. Lack of desire to socialize with colleagues outside of work as before the loss of a loved one.
5. Reports that thoughts are dominated by recent loss and he/she cannot focus on anything else for more than a few minutes at the most.
6. Avoids talking on anything but a superficial level about the loss.
7. Appears to be losing weight or/and experiencing insomnia since the loss.

—. _____
_____
—. _____
_____
—. _____
_____

LONG-TERM GOALS

1. Return to previous level of productivity, social functioning, and positive mood in the workplace.
2. Begin and sustain an emotional grieving process around the loss.
3. Develop an awareness of how the avoidance of grieving and the attempts to deny the loss has affected functioning at work as well as in all interpersonal relations.

4. Complete the formal grieving process by letting go of the debilitating symptoms associated with intense preoccupation with the lost significant other.

5. Regain an appreciation for and awareness of colleagues at work and outside the workplace.

6. Realize that, although the sense of loss of a loved one will never disappear and will always make him/her vulnerable to feelings of sadness and loss, he/she can again experience pleasure in other relationships and other aspects of life.

—. _____

    _____

—. _____

    _____

—. _____

    _____

SHORT-TERM OBJECTIVES

1. Identify the specific losses and articulate the emotional effects of the losses in functioning at work and at home. (1, 2)

2. Begin verbalizing feelings associated with the loss. (1, 2)

3. Tell the story of the loss, bringing pictures and memorabilia if available and appropriate. (1, 2, 3, 4, 9)

4. Identify the steps in the grieving process and describe his/her personal experience with the process. (2, 3, 4, 5, 6)

5. Verbalize whether he/she used substances to avoid

THERAPEUTIC INTERVENTIONS

1. Explore the causes of the grief reaction, encouraging the employee to tell the story with detail and feeling.

2. Using active and reflective listening skills, assist employee in clarifying and sharing feelings about the loss.

3. Explain to the employee that he/she is in the process of grieving and answer any questions he/she has about it.

4. Educate the employee on the stages of the grieving process.

5. Suggest the employee read *Living When A Loved One Has Died* (Grollman); *Good*

feelings associated with the loss. (7, 8)

6. Verbalize how avoiding feeling the pain associated with the loss has negatively impacted his/her functioning at work and at home. (7, 8)

7. Identify the positive things about the deceased loved one and/or the relationship and how these things may be remembered. (5, 9)

8. Acknowledge the strength of the attachment to the lost loved one and begin to gradually refocus activity on the future. (5, 10, 13, 18)

9. Verbalize feelings of anger or guilt focused on self or the deceased loved one that inhibits grief process. (11, 16, 18)

10. Increase productivity, regular work attendance, social interaction with coworkers, and focused concentration. (8, 12, 19)

11. Write a daily grief journal of feelings and thoughts regarding the loss. (13)

12. Give permission to EAP counselor to speak with coworkers regarding his/her grief. (12, 14)

13. Agree to speak to other grieving employees as the grief process resolves. (15)

14. Agree to accept a referral to a mental health provider for ongoing counseling. Give EAP permission for a release of information. (16, 17)

Grief (Westberg); *How Can It Be All Right When Everything Is All Wrong* (Smedes); *When Bad Things Happen To Good People* (Kushner); or another book on grief and loss.

6. If employee resists reading any of the preceding books, read aloud a portion of one that is most relevant for this specific employee and the situation at hand.

7. Explore the role of substance abuse in coping with the loss. If it is a factor, refer employee for complete evaluation and treatment.

8. Explore how grief has negatively affected employee's functioning at home and work.

9. Assist employee in recalling a list of positive memories of deceased loved one.

10. Gently and gradually encourage employee to focus on the positive aspects of living for the future in spite of the pain.

11. Explore employee's feelings of guilt or anger associated with the loss. If these feelings are severe, refer him/her immediately to a mental health provider.

12. Facilitate a supportive workplace by meeting with employee's coworkers and discussing the dynamics of grieving, often suggesting ways of interacting with the

15. Attend a grief support group. (18)

16. Cooperate with a referral to a physician for psychotropic medication evaluation. (19)

___. _____
   _____

___. _____
   _____

___. _____
   _____

employee and answering any questions they have about how to talk and relate to the employee.

13. Suggest employee keep a daily grief journal to be shared in therapy/support group setting.

14. Seek permission from the employee to talk with his/her department head about how coworkers should work with the employee to help him/her cope with the loss.

15. If appropriate, ask employee if he/she would be willing to speak to other employees in the future whose experience of losing a loved one is similar to his/her own circumstances.

16. Refer the employee to a counselor with specialty training in bereavement.

17. Obtain permission from employee to share pertinent information with the referring therapist/physician as well as follow up with the therapist to ensure that the referral suits the employee's needs.

18. Refer the employee to a bereavement support group.

19. If symptoms seriously compromise employee functioning, refer him/her to a physician for psychotropic medication evaluation.

—.   _____
     _____
—.   _____
     _____
—.   _____
     _____

DIAGNOSTIC SUGGESTIONS

Axis I: 296.2x   Major Depressive Disorder, Single Episode
              296.3x   Major Depressive Disorder, Recurrent
              309.0   Adjustment Disorder with Depressed Mood
              V62.82   Bereavement
              _____   _____
              _____   _____

LEGAL CONFLICTS

BEHAVIORAL DEFINITIONS

1. Making frequent appearances at court during business hours due to legal charges or dispositions pending.
2. History of repeated violations of the law, many of which occurred while under the influence of drugs or alcohol.
3. Distracted from focusing at work by legal pressures, such as a pending divorce, child custody suit, and/or struggle with relatives for power of attorney over an estate.
4. Ability to travel independently for the company limited by "Driving While Intoxicated" license restriction.
5. Fear of loss of job due to current legal charges and anxious preoccupation.
6. Unresolved legal problems complicating recovery from substance abuse.
7. Fear of legal system adjudicating current problems in a way that will negatively affect job status.
8. Court-ordered treatment for substance abuse.

—. _____
    _____
—. _____
    _____
—. _____
    _____

LONG-TERM GOALS

1. Respond to and accept the mandates of the court and consent to legal representation.

2. Understand how excessive alcohol consumption prior to driving has contributed to legal problems and accept the need to alter and improve this behavior.

3. Accept responsibility for decisions and actions that have led to legal problems without blaming others.

4. Maintain a program of recovery or moderate drinking which will minimize if not totally ameliorate substance abuse and legal problems.

5. Internalize the need for and value of treatment.

—. _____

_____

—. _____

_____

—. _____

_____

SHORT-TERM OBJECTIVES

1. Describe current legal problems and the circumstances that led to them. (1)

2. Verbalize and accept responsibility for the series of decisions and actions that eventually led to illegal activity. (1, 6)

3. Make regular contact with court officers to fulfill sentencing requirements. (2)

4. Communicate with manager and appropriate employees in human resources to ensure that they understand the desire and need to resolve legal problems. (3)

5. Negotiate with employer to find ways to satisfy the

THERAPEUTIC INTERVENTIONS

1. Probe the exact nature of employee's legal entanglements and the series of decisions that led to his/her behaving in a manner resulting in arrest.

2. Encourage employee to keep appointments with court officers or court referral programs.

3. Reinforce employee's need for a rehabilitation/treatment plan and resolution of legal problems while sustaining his/her employment status.

4. Explore issue of substance abuse and how it may have contributed to employee's legal conflict, emphasizing

needs of the court while continuing to make a contribution at work in order to remain gainfully employed. (3)

6. Maintain sobriety at work in accordance with the rules of the workplace. (4)

7. Maintain sobriety in accordance with the rules of probation/parole. (5)

8. Verbalize an acceptance of responsibility for substance abuse and its relationship to legal problems without blaming others. (6)

9. Verbalize the powerlessness and unmanageability that result from legal conflicts and substance abuse. (4)

10. Meet with an attorney to make plans for resolving legal conflicts. (8)

11. Keep all conditions of probation/parole. (9)

12. Actively participate in a rehabilitation/treatment program. (5, 10, 11)

13. Sign a release of information from treatment provider to EAP representative to aid in coordination of treatment plan with work duties. (12, 13)

14. Actively participate in an ongoing aftercare program. (11, 13, 14)

15. Actively attend AA/NA support groups. (15)

16. Maintain sobriety while driving in accordance with

the necessity for sobriety at work.

5. Refer employee to a substance abuse treatment program and/or AA meetings. Monitor follow-through.

6. Confront employee's denial of substance abuse by reviewing various negative consequence of his/her drug use.

7. Help employee understand the relationship between substance abuse and legal conflicts and explore how these problems result in powerlessness and unmanageability.

8. Encourage and facilitate the employee meeting with an attorney to discuss plans for resolving legal conflicts.

9. Check written court documents to see that employee is meeting all conditions of his/her probation/parole.

10. Provide support while employee is engaged in rehabilitation program.

11. Follow up with employee as to his/her appointment compliance with treatment.

12. Get written permission from employee to receive information from treatment provider regarding his/her treatment planning that will be helpful to coordinate his/her ongoing work responsibilities.

13. Review employee's ongoing treatment plan.

laws or probation/parole. (14, 16)

17. Articulate and demonstrate the values that affirm behavior within the boundaries of the law. (17, 18)

__. _____
   _____

__. _____
   _____

__. _____
   _____

14. Monitor and reinforce employee treatment and parole/probation compliance.

15. Support employee's attendance at AA/NA support groups.

16. Urge and encourage driving only when completely clean and sober.

17. Support employee's need to obey workplace laws, policies, and procedures, as well as probation/parole requirements.

18. Help employee understand the importance of resolving legal conflicts honestly.

__. _____
   _____

__. _____
   _____

__. _____
   _____

DIAGNOSTIC SUGGESTIONS

Axis I: 312.8   Conduct Disorder
            313.81   Oppositional Defiant Disorder
            309.3   Adjustment Disorder With Disturbance of Conduct
            303.90   Alcohol Dependence
            305.00   Alcohol Abuse
            V71.01   Adult Antisocial Behavior

            _____   _____

Axis II: 301.7   Antisocial Personality Disorder
            301.83   Borderline Personality Disorder

            _____   _____
            _____   _____

LOW SELF-ESTEEM

BEHAVIORAL DEFINITIONS

1. Fails to defend self when challenged/questioned about his or her work product.
2. States a dislike for self and his/her work.
3. Makes self-disparaging remarks and takes blame easily.
4. Unkempt grooming, slovenly appearance, and minimal eye contact.
5. Avoids challenging assignments from his/her manager.
6. Stops contributing positively to the work situation after a colleague gives him/her a compliment or questions the value of his/her contribution.
7. Acquiesces to the requests of coworkers to undertake tasks even though they have failed to meet the individual targets and deadlines that the manager has set for them.

—. _____
_____
—. _____
_____
—. _____
_____

LONG-TERM GOALS

1. Possess a degree of self-esteem that fuels his/her ability to both enjoy life and assert self positively both at home and work.
2. Develop and sustain a consistent positive self-image.

3. Demonstrate improved self-esteem through pride in appearance, greater eye contact, and identification of positive traits in self-talk messages.
4. Develop ability to defend self at work and to disagree with an authority figure who questions his/her work inputs.

—. _____

   _____

   _____

—. _____

   _____

   _____

—. _____

   _____

SHORT-TERM OBJECTIVES

1. Increase awareness of self-disparaging statements. (1)
2. Identify positive things about self. (2, 3, 4)
3. Decrease frequency of negative self-statements and increase frequency of positive statements about self. (2, 3, 4)
4. Identify negative self-talk messages used to reinforce low self-esteem. (4, 5)
5. Report instances of using positive self-talk messages to build self-esteem. (3, 6)
6. Identify positive things about work. (7, 8)
7. Decrease the frequency of negative, critical, complaintive statements about job or his/her ability to do it well and increase the frequency of positive statements. (7, 8)

THERAPEUTIC INTERVENTIONS

1. Confront and probe employee's self-disparaging comments.
2. Ask employee to list his/her positive traits and talents and to keep list in pocket for frequent review throughout the day.
3. Reinforce employee's positive self-talk and self-descriptive statements.
4. Recommend employee read Burns' *Ten Days to Self-Esteem* and *The Feeling Good Handbook*. Review application of the principles in these books to his/her life.
5. Assist employee in identifying the negative messages he/she gives to self that foster low self-esteem and a lack of confidence.
6. Role-play instances of employee giving self-

8. Increase frequency of assertive behaviors. (9)

9. Identify tasks that can be done to improve self-image and a plan to achieve those goals. (10)

10. Verbalize insight into the historical and current sources of low self-esteem. (11, 12)

11. Increase understanding and verbalize awareness of how feelings of worthlessness often relate to feelings and reactions toward parental figures. (11, 12)

12. Arrive for work showing evidence of improved daily grooming and personal hygiene. (13)

13. Positively acknowledge verbal compliments from others without self-disparagement or withdrawal. (14, 15)

14. Take verbal responsibility for accomplishments without minimizing efforts, inputs, or outcomes. (3, 6, 8, 14, 15)

15. Identify those situations that trigger fears of failure and state the positive self-talk that will be used to counteract the fear. (16)

16. Initiate conversations with manager and colleagues about matters of concern and participate in informal social banter. (17)

17. Accept referral to psychotherapist for further evalua-

positive encouraging messages about abilities, worth, and contribution to work, home, friends, or family.

7. Assign employee the task of listing the positive aspects of his/her job and keeping list in pocket for frequent review throughout the day.

8. Encourage and reinforce employee's positive statements about work and his/her contribution.

9. Refer employee to support group that is focused on assertiveness training.

10. Assist employee in identifying a series of small steps that could be taken in work or personal life to build confidence and self-esteem by periodically inquiring about his/her reaction to the counseling session.

11. Probe the origins of employee's negative self-concept.

12. Explore whether employee's low self-esteem may be based in negative messages from parents and/or guilt as a reaction to angry feelings toward them.

13. Confront employee's lack of attention to personal appearance and ask what specific actions he/she could take to improve hygiene and grooming habits.

14. Explore the basis for the employee's fear of being

tion and ongoing counseling as necessary to improve self-esteem. (18, 19)

—. _____
_____

—. _____
_____

—. _____
_____

taken seriously as an active and competent professional.

15. Have employee role-play accepting a compliment and giving self-positive affirmation with the compliment.

16. During follow-up with employee on the job, help him/her articulate triggers to vulnerable feeling states and reinforce and articulate strategies to bolster and mobilize confidence.

17. Help employee understand the need to actively participate in and guide his/her career and work situation by seeking out opportunities to converse with colleagues and superiors and contribute to the goals in the workplace.

18. Refer employee to psychotherapist for formal psychological evaluation and ongoing supportive and exploratory psychotherapy.

19. Motivate employee to follow up with psychotherapist for ongoing assistance by periodically inquiring about his/her reaction to the counseling session.

—. _____
_____

—. _____
_____

—. _____
_____

DIAGNOSTIC SUGGESTIONS

Axis I: 300.23   Social Phobia
          300.4   Dysthymic Disorder
          296.xx   Major Depressive Disorder

          _____   _____

Axis II: 301.83   Borderline Personality Disorder

          _____   _____

          _____   _____

MANAGER ROLE CONFLICT

BEHAVIORAL DEFINITIONS

1. Fear of promotion to managerial position.
2. Feelings of depression or anxiety with regard to authority and/or leadership role.
3. Difficulty in giving critical feedback to supervisees.
4. Difficulty in maintaining relationships with former peers in non-management positions or feelings of loss connected with those relationships.

—. _____

_____

—. _____

_____

—. _____

_____

LONG-TERM GOALS

1. Improved satisfaction and comfort in role as manager.
2. Increase sense of confidence and competence in acting in a leadership role.
3. Be able to give critical feedback to employees to improve their performance.
4. Be able to coach and mentor employees.
5. Establish friendships within managerial peer group.
6. Solidify friendships with former peers in nonmanagement positions.
7. Successfully step out of managerial role into another job or career path.

——. _____
_____
——. _____
_____
——. _____
_____

SHORT-TERM OBJECTIVES

1. Describe nature of conflicts connected to assuming or maintaining a management position. (1)

2. Place conflicts connected to management role in a historical context. (2)

3. Identify sources of conflict with authority or leadership role stemming from relationships with significant authority figures in his/her past. (3)

4. Identify costs and benefits in assuming or maintaining a management position. (4, 5)

5. Identify specific behavioral changes necessary for successful functioning in a managerial role. (6, 7)

6. Prioritize, if necessary, behavioral changes necessary for success in managerial role. (8)

7. Identify sources of training and education for management position. (9)

THERAPEUTIC INTERVENTIONS

1. Clarify the nature of the conflicts surrounding managerial role.

2. Solicit career history with particular attention to how promotion to managerial position took place, and the history of any managerial training.

3. Ask for description of significant authority figures (managers) in employee's life, including parents, teachers, and former managers.

4. Solicit employee's career goals.

5. Have employee list the pros and cons of accepting or maintaining a management position.

6. Ask employee to describe characteristics of an ideal manager.

7. Have employee rate the importance of characteristics necessary to the successful manager, from most important to least important.

8. Enroll in management education and training programs. (10)

9. Ask a successful manager to act as mentor or coach. (11, 12, 13)

10. Identify irrational cognitions connected with difficulty in assuming or maintaining management position. (14, 15)

11. Develop and practice healthier, more realistic cognitions that promote success in management role. (16)

12. Initiate practice of assertiveness skills that will facilitate the provision of constructive feedback to employees without aggression or defensiveness. (17, 18)

13. Demonstrate ability to verbalize specific behavioral descriptions of job performance problems and required job performance changes for use in performance review situations. (19)

14. Evaluate finding a new, nonmanagement position inside or outside of current corporation. (20)

___. _____
    _____

___. _____
    _____

___. _____
    _____

8. Ask employee to rate him-/herself on a 10-point scale on selected characteristics of the ideal manager.

9. Have employee bring in information about corporate-sponsored training programs available to managers and then discuss and evaluate them.

10. Help employee select and enroll in management training program(s) and review.

11. Inquire about corporate-sponsored mentoring or coaching programs.

12. Ask employee to identify successful managers that may serve as a mentor or coach.

13. Have employee script and role-play asking a successful manager to serve as mentor or coach.

14. Demonstrate role that irrational beliefs may play in promoting negative and self-defeating emotions and behaviors.

15. Solicit from employee irrational beliefs that lead to negative and self-defeating emotions and behaviors.

16. Script rational self-dialogue that promotes increased feelings of competence in managerial role.

17. Train employee in assertiveness skills or refer him/her to an assertiveness training class.

18. Role-play giving assertive feedback to an employee, making an assertive request for a behavioral change, and providing clear, enforceable consequences should job performance not change.

19. Demonstrate for manager how to operationally define ambiguous, problematic, vague employee attributes and processes as concrete behaviors that can be measured and changed.

20. Discuss and evaluate job-change strategies.

___. _____
    _____
___. _____
    _____
___. _____
    _____

DIAGNOSTIC SUGGESTIONS

Axis I:	300.4	Dysthymic Disorder
	309.24	Adjustment Disorder With Anxiety
	309.0	Adjustment Disorder With Depressed Mood
	_____	_____
	_____	_____
Axis II:	301.81	Narcissistic Personality Disorder
	301.9	Personality Disorder NOS
	301.7	Antisocial Personality Disorder
	_____	_____
	_____	_____

MANAGERIAL CONFLICT

BEHAVIORAL DEFINITIONS

1. Frequent or continual disagreements or arguments with manager that may have led to workplace disciplinary action or a stall in career development.
2. Lack of communication with manager.
3. Passive noncompliance in response to manager's requests.
4. Refusal to follow manager's directives or work assignments (insubordination).
5. Refusal to make eye contact with manager.
6. Physical and/or verbal provocation of manager or use of aggressive language and gestures in response to manager.
7. Initiates and provokes discussions with coworkers aimed at spreading negative or inflammatory information about manager.
8. A pattern of angry projection of responsibility for ongoing conflict on manager.

—. _____
   _____
—. _____
   _____
—. _____
   _____

LONG-TERM GOALS

1. Increase awareness of his/her role in beginning and/or perpetuating conflict with the manager.
2. Develop ability to resolve disagreements with the manager in a mature, controlled, nonaggressive, and/or assertive manner.

3. Develop mutual respect in the employee-manager relationship.
4. Comply in a timely and positive manner with the manager's requests.
5. Cease attempts to persuade or manipulate coworkers into hostile relationships with the manager.
6. Appropriately and maturely end relationship with the manager by finding a new position inside or outside of current workplace.

—. _____

_____

—. _____

_____

—. _____

_____

SHORT-TERM OBJECTIVES

1. Verbalize the issues that surround the conflict with the manager. (1)
2. Comply with and resolve current disciplinary status. (2)
3. List escalating behaviors in conflict with manager. (3, 4)
4. Identify own possible role in provoking or maintaining conflict. (1, 3, 4)
5. Enumerate personal changes that could improve relationship with the manager. (3, 4, 5)
6. Identify potential costs versus benefits of continuing the conflict with the manager. Verbalize a conclusion that conflict resolution is necessary. (6)

THERAPEUTIC INTERVENTION

1. Ask employee to explain history of conflict with manager from the point of view of a neutral observer.
2. If employee is currently on disciplinary status connected to conflict with manager, ask him/her to bring in related documents for joint review.
3. Ask employee to make a list of escalating behaviors that commonly occur in his/her interactions with manager.
4. Confront employee's avoidance of responsibility for conflict with manager.
5. Assign employee the task of listing changes he/she needs to make to improve relationship with manager. Process list.

7. State the behavioral alternatives that can be used when frustration or anger with the manager builds. (4, 7)

8. Verbalize the difference between assertive and aggressive behavior. (8, 9)

9. Identify patterns of conflict with authority figures. (4, 10)

10. Verbalize how this particular conflict fits the pattern of dissatisfaction and anger with authority figures generally. (10, 11)

11. Verbalize a need to change own attitude regarding managerial authority generally. (11, 12)

12. Identify and display understanding of the link between cognition about the manager and resultant feelings. (13, 14)

13. Identify and verbalize mutual workplace goals for self and manager. (15)

14. Verbalize an awareness and understanding of the benefit of forgiving the manager. (16)

15. Initiate neutral or positive verbal interaction with manager at least one time per day. (13, 14, 17, 18)

16. Report an increase in the frequency of positive business communication with the manager. (17, 18, 19)

6. Have employee list advantages and disadvantages of continuing in conflict with manager and then urge conflict resolution.

7. Jointly examine alternative behavioral responses to hostile interactions with manager.

8. Explain, differentiate, and model differences between assertive and aggressive behavior.

9. Refer employee to an assertiveness training group and/or assign reading on the topic (e.g., *Your Perfect Right,* by Albert and Emmons).

10. Review and process similar instances of conflict with authority figures in employee's past.

11. Confront employee on how this specific conflict fits his/her pattern of conflict with authority figures or a critical attitude regarding management.

12. Reinforce employee's acceptance of a need to change his/her attitude of discontent with others who are in a decision-making position.

13. Demonstrate for employee the role that irrational expectations and beliefs play in hostile feelings and responses to manager.

14. Script self-talk dialogue for employee that promotes an

17. Request, arrange, and actively participate in conflict resolution exercises or seminars. (20)

18. List costs and benefits of remaining in current position. (21)

19. Evaluate possibility of finding a new job inside or outside current corporation. (22)

—. _____
_____

—. _____
_____

—. _____
_____

even-tempered response to the manager.

15. Ask employee to make a hypothetical list of the weekly, monthly, or year-long goals the manager needs to fulfill.

16. Discuss with employee the rationale for forgiveness. Recommend for reading, *Forgive and Forget* (Smedes).

17. Assign employee the task of approaching manager and initiating nonconflictual communication at least once per day before next visit.

18. Use role play, behavioral rehearsal, and modeling to teach employee conflict resolution and positive verbal interaction with the manager.

19. Reinforce employee's reports of positive interaction with manager.

20. Ask employee to determine the availability of conflict-resolution programs within or outside the workplace (e.g., training department, outside consultants, executive coaches, seminars, and/or community resources).

21. Ask employee to discuss positives and negatives connected with continuing in present employment position.

22. Discuss and evaluate job-
change strategies.

___. _____
      _____

___. _____
      _____

___. _____
      _____

DIAGNOSTIC SUGGESTIONS

Axis I:

300.4	Dysthymic Disorder
309.0	Adjustment Disorder With Depressed Mood
309.3	Adjustment Disorder With Disturbance of Conduct
309.4	Adjustment Disorder With Mixed Disturbance of Emotions and Conduct
312.8	Conduct Disorder
312.34	Intermittent Explosive Disorder
V71.01	Adult Antisocial Behavior
_____	_____

Axis II:

301.81	Narcissistic Personality Disorder
301.0	Paranoid Personality Disorder
301.83	Borderline Personality Disorder
301.7	Antisocial Personality Disorder
301.9	Personality Disorder NOS
_____	_____
_____	_____

MANAGERIAL DEFICIENCIES

BEHAVIORAL DEFINITIONS

1. Frustrated attempts to help employee result in failure to confront late attendance or deteriorating work performance.
2. Overidentification with the employee and his/her problem and failure to intervene with unsatisfactory performance.
3. Gets angry at employee and expects more of him/her than others within the unit.
4. Denies that a problem exists even though coworkers have mentioned the worker's deficiencies and problematic behavior.
5. Ignores obvious ongoing conflict between employees without attempting to resolve the friction.

__. _____
    _____
__. _____
    _____
__. _____
    _____

LONG-TERM GOALS

1. Actively address employee patterns of deteriorating performance, unusual behavior, or interpersonal conflict.
2. Become proactive and assertive in dealing with personnel problems in a constructive, evenhanded, effective manner.
3. Counsel each of the department's employees regarding his/her performance review within the appropriate time lines set by management.

4. Perform a self-assessment of skills and performance, identifying areas that need future development.
5. Ensure that each employee has clear delineation of job roles and responsibilities.
6. Implement coaching techniques in personnel management: a methodology consisting of counseling, monitoring, educating, and confronting.
7. Realize that most employees who work for the company do so primarily out of necessity to make a living, and the manager's primary role is to manage and lead employees in their job tasks—not befriend, protect, coverup for, or abuse them.
8. As appropriate, contact human resource representative for consultation regarding any employee relations issue affecting or involving employees within the department, such as sexual harassment, age discrimination, Americans with Disabilities Act (ADA), etc.

__. _____
_____
__. _____
_____
__. _____
_____

SHORT-TERM OBJECTIVES

1. Describe, in general, the personnel problems that exist and management actions that have been taken to address these problems. (1)

2. Document the specific nature of the employee problem, its length, duration, intensity, how it has impacted on employee performance, and what needs to be done for the problem to be resolved. (1, 2)

THERAPEUTIC INTERVENTIONS

1. Assist manager in delineating the exact nature of his/her department's personnel problems and what attempts he/she has made to resolve them.

2. Assist manager with the protocols and forms to use to document issues surrounding problem employee.

3. Discuss, explore, and assist manager in identifying who else within the company should be consulted regarding actions to be taken in

3. Ask a human resource representative to review the written documentation and solicit his/her comments or suggestions. (2, 3)

4. Identify the biases, beliefs, values, or personality characteristics that are affecting his/her ability to objectively deal with the situation. (4, 5)

5. Identify successful techniques used personally or witnessed in the past that may be useful in this situation. (6)

6. Report the realization that he/she has not dealt with all employees equally and this inequity has created additional conflict within the department. (5, 7, 8)

7. Agree to an action plan designed to resolve immediate employee problem. (9)

8. Identify expected employee resistance to the action plan and the stress that will result from responding to that resistance. (10)

9. Acknowledge own resistance and avoidance behaviors that will arise and identify steps to deal with that resistance. (11, 12)

10. Carry out action plan. (13)

11. Report back to the EAP to discuss how implementation of action plan is going. (11, 14)

12. Accept a referral to mental health professional to relation to problem employee.

4. Assist manager in identifying his/her personal traits, values, and beliefs that are influencing his/her judgment and behavior in relation to the personnel problem.

5. Assist the manager in a review of the differences between the roles of manager and friend within the workplace.

6. Review manager's evolution and work history with a focus on understanding what skills and techniques have worked best for him/her or other managers and what have not.

7. Suggest the manager review and compare his/her behavior toward problem employee and other employees in the department.

8. Discuss with manager consequences of "letting the rules bend."

9. Develop an action plan with manager that deals directly with employee problem and terminates his/her pattern of avoidance or inequality in management approach.

10. Help manager anticipate what resistance there might be on the part of the employee and perhaps the organization to the action plan and develop a constructive response to this resistance.

deal with personal issues that interfere with professional management effectiveness. (15)

13. Develop a list of key actions that are essential to focus on when managing and motivating employees. (16)

—. _____
_____

—. _____
_____

—. _____
_____

11. Encourage manager to verbalize his/her own resistance to the action plan and develop a plan to deal with avoidance of implementation (e.g., accountability to EAP director and/or setting implementation deadlines).

12. Help manager understand the etiology of his/her resistance to implementing the action plan.

13. Set implementation date and discuss the sequence of steps to be taken. Use role play and modeling to teach specific communication, problem resolution, and assertiveness skills.

14. Monitor action plan implementation, noting need for follow-through and consistency by manager.

15. If indicated, refer the manager to a mental health professional for comprehensive evaluation.

16. Help manager evaluate other progressive measures he/she may take to insure that the department is managed fairly, effectively, and efficiently.

—. _____
_____

—. _____
_____

—. _____
_____

DIAGNOSTIC SUGGESTIONS

Axis I: 309.24   Adjustment Disorder With Anxiety
309.0   Adjustment Disorder With Depressed Mood
309.4   Adjustment Disorder With Mixed Disturbance
             of Emotions and Conduct
313.82   Identity Problem

_____   _____

Axis II: 301.83   Borderline Personality Disorder
301.7   Antisocial Personality Disorder
301.9   Personality Disorder NOS

_____   _____

_____   _____

MARITAL CONFLICT

BEHAVIORAL DEFINITIONS

1. Arguments with spouse that cause preoccupation and detract from work performance.
2. Lack of marital communication which results in frustration and anger.
3. Avoidance of home life due to stress in the marital relationship.
4. Excessive time spent at work as a means of avoiding contact with spouse.
5. Pending separation due to the inability to experience pleasure in the marriage.
6. Increased irritability, sleeplessness, depression, and social withdrawal as a result of marital stress.
7. A pattern of angry responses to manager, which appears to be a displacement and projection of conflict with the spouse.
8. The stress of a divorce proceeding leading to periods of tearfulness and low energy at work.

—. _____
   _____

—. _____
   _____

—. _____
   _____

LONG-TERM GOALS

1. Develop more effective coping techniques to deal with feelings surrounding the marital conflict.

2. Select a marriage counselor and attend sessions in an attempt to resolve conflict.
3. Return to previous level of effective functioning as a productive employee without preoccupation with relationship problem.
4. Resolve conflicts and develop mutual respect for significant other in the relationship.
5. Increase understanding of own role in the relationship conflicts.
6. Develop the ability to handle marital conflicts in a controlled, nonaggressive, and assertive manner.
7. Accept the irreconcilable differences in the relationship and its eventual termination.
8. Learn to identify escalating behaviors that lead to increased conflict.
9. Develop and practice the necessary skills for effective, open, mutually satisfying communication and intimacy.

—. _____
   _____
   _____
—. _____
   _____
   _____
—. _____
   _____

SHORT-TERM OBJECTIVES

1. Identify and describe the present conflicts with spouse. (1)
2. List the activities undertaken to resolve the conflicts. (2)
3. Identify and discuss understanding of the causes of the conflict. (3)
4. Identify future plans regarding spouse. (4)
5. Acknowledge own role in relationship conflict and what he/she could do to improve the relationship. (5, 6)

THERAPEUTIC INTERVENTIONS

1. Engage the employee by exploring the extent and duration of the conflicts.
2. Review employee's efforts to try to resolve marital problems.
3. Ask the employee about his/her understanding of the root causes of the conflicts.
4. Assess employee's motivation by asking if he/she is committed to resolving the conflict with spouse.

6. Attend assertiveness training classes to increase conflict-coping ability and communication effectiveness. (7)

7. Identify the issues and behaviors that escalate the levels of conflict with spouse. (8)

8. Terminate escalating behaviors as they are destructive to conflict resolution. (9)

9. Use "I messages" in communication with spouse to reduce blaming and defensiveness. (10)

10. Bring the spouse into the EAP for consultation regarding the problem. (11)

11. Make appointments with mental health professionals for an initial consultation. (12, 13)

12. Talk openly and honestly to the counselors about the problems. (14)

13. Ask each counselor about the counseling process as to what is expected of the couple, what is the counselor's style or role, and how a treatment plan would be developed. (15)

14. Discuss initial impressions of and reactions to the counselor with the EAP. (16)

15. Decide on which counselor to see on a regular basis to resolve marital conflict. (17)

5. Ask employee to evaluate his/her own contribution to the problems in the relationship.

6. Assist employee in listing behaviors he/she could change to increase spouse's level of happiness.

7. Refer employee to an assertiveness training class.

8. Assist employee in identifying behaviors that escalate the level of conflict with spouse and destroy effective problem resolution.

9. Encourage termination of escalating behaviors.

10. Use modeling or role playing to teach the use of "I messages" that express feelings about but avoid blaming partner.

11. Encourage the employee to bring his/her spouse in for a conjoint interview to more fully assess the nature of the problems.

12. Suggest a referral to two mental health professionals to help them solve the conflicts. Suggest they visit each to evaluate degree of comfort with and confidence in each.

13. Help employee anticipate what the interview consultation with the mental health professional may be like.

16. Make a series of appointments with the selected counselor. (18)
17. Attend sessions with the counselor. (19)
18. Report back to EAP regarding the status of the marital conflict. (20)

__. _____
   _____
__. _____
   _____
__. _____
   _____

14. Encourage the employee to attend the mental health consultations and talk openly about his/her marital conflicts.
15. Encourage the employee to ask specific questions about how the process would proceed and the counselor's approach or style.
16. Determine a time and method to discuss how the employee felt about each of the EAP-referred mental health professionals.
17. Assist employee in deciding which mental health professional might be the best fit for the couple to resolve the problem.
18. Encourage the employee to begin counseling on a regular basis.
19. Determine with employee when and how to follow up to determine whether this is the appropriate modality of treatment and the appropriate therapist.
20. Offer ongoing support during the counseling process.

__. _____
   _____
__. _____
   _____
__. _____
   _____

DIAGNOSTIC SUGGESTIONS

Axis I: 300.4   Dysthymic Disorder
309.0   Adjustment Disorder with Depressed Mood
V61.1   Partner Relational Problem
V62.81   Relational Problem NOS

———   ——————————————

———   ——————————————

Axis II: 301.9   Personality Disorder NOS
301.81   Narcissistic Personality Disorder

———   ——————————————

———   ——————————————

MEDICAL PROBLEM

BEHAVIORAL DEFINITIONS

1. A diagnosed medical condition that affects attendance, productivity, or behavior in the workplace (e.g., hypertension, asthma, diabetes, heart disease, low back disorders, cancer, and/or AIDS)
2. A serious and debilitating medical condition that terminates ability to perform work responsibilities and leads to disability status.
3. Difficult or complicated pregnancy.
4. A chronic medical condition exacerbated by workplace stress.
5. Constant pain, frequent headaches, constant tiredness, or feeling generally unwell that results in frequent absenteeism.
6. Psychological or behavioral factors that negatively influence the course of a medical condition.

—. _____
_____
_____
—. _____
_____
_____
—. _____
_____

LONG-TERM GOALS

1. Medically stabilize physical condition.
2. Alleviate acute medical condition.
3. Accept impact of chronic physical condition on career, making realistic accommodations where necessary.
4. Tolerate, accommodate, and accept chronic physical symptoms connected to diagnosed medical condition.

5. Make application for disability and accept a plan for long-term treatment, rehabilitation, and a change in lifestyle.
6. Understand the role that psychological and behavioral factors play in the development or exacerbation of medical condition and resolve the debilitating interaction.
7. Learn efficient coping strategies for environmental stressors that contribute to the development or exacerbation of the medical condition.

—. _____
_____

—. _____
_____

—. _____
_____

SHORT-TERM OBJECTIVES

1. Comply with physician's orders for tests, medications, limitations, and/or treatments. (1, 2, 4)

2. Demonstrate responsibility by taking prescribed medication(s) consistently and on time. (2)

3. Develop contingency steps for follow-up medical care should medical condition change. (2, 4)

4. Report any symptoms experienced or medication side effects to physician or therapist. (2)

5. Demonstrate accurate and thorough knowledge of medical condition. (3, 4, 5)

6. Increase knowledge of how proper nutrition and other

THERAPEUTIC INTERVENTIONS

1. Refer employee to physician (or into employee's health plan) for physical examination.

2. Monitor and document employee's follow-through on physician's orders and redirect when employee is failing to comply.

3. Ask employee to describe medical condition and evaluate the accuracy of understanding of the medical problem and the plan for treatment/rehabilitation.

4. Reinforce and assist employee in securing appropriate and necessary treatment in employee's medical plan (e.g., nutrition consults, physical therapy, medical specialists).

positive lifestyle behaviors (e.g., exercise) can have a positive impact on medical condition. (4, 5)

7. Comply with corporate disability program requirements. (6, 7)

8. Identify emotions prior to and in reaction to medical condition. (8)

9. Identify how emotions and cognitions may produce a negative impact on health. (9, 10)

10. Make a commitment to try to keep self in a positive emotional state as a means of promoting healing. (10, 11)

11. Identify workplace and other environmental stressors that exacerbate physical symptoms of medical condition. (12)

12. Discuss and verbally commit to the use of new coping strategies for workplace and other environmental stressors that have exacerbated medical condition. (9, 10, 13, 14)

13. Decrease level of denial regarding medical condition while increasing level of verbal acceptance. (2, 3, 15)

14. Discuss and verbally accept transition to full-time disability status. (6, 16)

15. Attend a support group related to the medical condition. (11, 10, 17)

5. Solicit from employee and/or offer explanation as to how lifestyle factors (e.g., drinking, exercise, sleep pattern) negatively affect medical condition.

6. Assign employee (or assist if necessary) task of contacting human resource or line manager to gather information on corporate disability program.

7. Monitor and document employee's follow-through with requirements for compliance with corporate disability program.

8. Ask employee to identify and express feelings that predated and resulted from the medical condition.

9. Demonstrate the connection between irrational cognition and stressful emotional states.

10. Teach employee how negative emotional state (e.g., worry, anger, resentment, depression) that results from distorted cognitions can have a detrimental effect on physical health.

11. Encourage and reinforce positive emotions (e.g., relaxation, laughter, joy, pleasure, contentment) as a means of promoting physical healing.

12. Ask employee to examine and explain how career choice and workplace fac-

___. _____
      _____

___. _____
      _____

___. _____
      _____

tors may have interacted with medical condition.

13. Jointly examine alternative behavioral responses (e.g., relaxation procedure, physical exercise, shorter work hours, more diversions in lifestyle) to workplace stressors.

14. Train employee in focused breathing, mindfulness, meditation, or relaxation skills.

15. Confront employee's destructive denial of medical condition that prevents obtaining necessary treatment or recognizing work limitations.

16. Ask employee to determine personal criteria for moving into long-term disability status.

17. Help employee find, and reinforce attendance at, a support group related to his/her medical condition and process the employee's reaction to attending the group.

___. _____
      _____

___. _____
      _____

___. _____
      _____

DIAGNOSTIC SUGGESTIONS

Axis I:

300.81	Undifferentiated Somatoform Disorder
300.7	Hypochondriasis
307.80	Pain Disorder Associated With Psychological Factors
307.89	Pain Disorder Associated With Both Psychological Factors and an [Axis III Disorder]
303.90	Alcohol Dependence
304.20	Cocaine Dependence
316	Maladaptive Health Behaviors Affecting [Axis III Disorder]
316	Personality Traits Affecting [Axis III Disorder]
316	Psychological Factors Affecting [Axis III Disorder]
———	————————————————
———	————————————————

PARENT-CHILD CONFLICT

BEHAVIORAL DEFINITIONS

1. Consistent or frequent conflict with oppositional child in home.
2. Suspicion or knowledge of child's drug use.
3. Stress related to threatened or actual runaway incident(s) by child.
4. Worried about child truant from school.
5. Difficulty with enforcement of appropriate discipline in the home.
6. Admits to overprotection of his/her child.

___. _____

_____

___. _____

_____

___. _____

_____

LONG-TERM GOALS

1. Decrease level and frequency of conflict between parent and child.
2. Develop a closer, more caring relationship between parent and child.
3. Increase feelings of parenting competency.
4. Establish appropriate parental control in home.
5. Increase parent-child communication.
6. Allow child age-appropriate independence.

___. _____

_____

—. _____

    _____

    _____

—. _____

    _____

SHORT-TERM OBJECTIVES

1. Describe conflicts with child with attention to behavioral precipitants and consequences. (1, 2)

2. Discontinue any verbally and/or physically abusive punishment of child(ren) by any parent or child caregiver. (3, 4, 5, 6, 7)

3. Verbalize parental role in the establishment and communication of family rules and consequences. (8, 15)

4. Report on objective observations and monitoring of behavioral evidence of child's drug use. (9)

5. Acknowledge honestly (without denial) child's pattern of drug use. (10, 23)

6. Accept referral to and participate in substance abuse treatment for child. (11)

7. Accept referral for a psychological assessment of child and participate in any recommended treatment. (12, 13)

8. Accept referral for a psychoeducational assessment of child. (14, 29)

THERAPEUTIC INTERVENTIONS

1. Process parent-child conflicts and their causes.

2. Ask employee to narrate individual conflict incidents with attention to behaviors that led up to conflict, behaviors during conflict, and outcomes for all parties.

3. Ask employee for description of disciplinary techniques by both parents and/or caregivers.

4. Review with employee the definition of and the damage resulting from verbal abuse.

5. Confront employee's verbal and physical abuse or overly punitive methods of discipline and encourage him/her to cease them.

6. Inform employee of counselor's duty to report to legal authorities instances of child abuse.

7. Inform appropriate state or local authority of child abuse.

8. Confront employee when he/she is not taking responsibility for self in parent-child conflict.

9. Establish appropriate boundaries, develop clear rules, and follow through consistently with consequences for misbehavior. (15, 16, 23, 25)

10. Establish and provide records of a behavioral management system in the home that includes a reward system or a contingency contract. (17, 18, 19, 20)

11. Increase the frequency of praise and positive reinforcement for the child. Recall instances where positive reinforcements were used. (18)

12. Decrease harsh and punitive disciplinary practices. Report instances where anger was controlled and the techniques used to do so. (19, 21, 22)

13. Seek support and advice from parents in similar situations by joining a self-help group. (24)

14. Increase time spent with child in mutually enjoyable activities. (26, 27, 28)

15. Increase time spent with child by the uninvolved or detached parent in leisure, school, or work activities. (26)

16. Establish partnership through regular contacts with key figures in child's school (e.g., principal, teacher, counselor) to monitor and intervene in aca-

9. Review with employee behavioral signs and symptoms of drug use.

10. Confront employee's refusal to accept child's probable drug abuse and the need for a substance abuse evaluation and/or treatment.

11. Refer employee within health plan or to a community resource for a substance abuse evaluation and/or treatment for the child.

12. Refer employee within health plan or to a community resource for a psychological assessment of the child.

13. Refer employee within health plan or to a community resource for individual treatment for the child or family therapy.

14. Refer employee for psychoeducational evaluation of the child to rule out a learning disability that may be contributing to the impulsivity and acting out behaviors in school (note: Most medical benefit plans do not cover such evaluations).

15. Assist employee in verbalizing and documenting clear rules for children in the home.

16. Assist employee in increasing structure in the home to help child learn to delay gratification for longer-term goals (e.g., complete

demic progress and attendance issues. (29)

17. Increase communication on nonconflictual subjects between parent and child. (27, 28)

18. Verbalize knowledge of how overprotectiveness or family enmeshment is motivated by irrational fears. (30, 31, 32)

19. Increase the frequency and duration of time child is permitted to engage in age-appropriate activities independent of parents. (33)

—. _____
    _____

—. _____
    _____

—. _____
    _____

homework or chores before playing basketball or watching TV).

17. Design with employee a reward system and/or a behavioral contract to use in the home to reinforce identified positive behaviors on child's part and to deter impulsive or prohibited ones.

18. Encourage employee to provide frequent praise and positive reinforcement for child's positive behaviors and good impulse control.

19. Assist parents in understanding the technique and development of a time-out procedure to reinforce limits.

20. Monitor and reinforce employee's use of new behavioral management techniques, giving feedback and suggesting adjustments as needed.

21. Explain how meditational and self-control strategies (e.g., rational self-talk, present-focus, mindfulness) can enable employee to avoid losing temper and punitively or harshly disciplining child.

22. Suggest employee read the book, *How To Keep Your C.O.O.L. with Your Children,* by Makarowski.

23. Educate employee in the dynamics of enabling and tough love.

24. Refer employee to self-help group for parents (e.g., Parents Anonymous, Parents Without Partners).

25. Encourage and challenge employee not to continue protecting child from legal consequences of antisocial behaviors.

26. Give a directive to uninvolved or disengaged parent(s) to spend more time with child in leisure, school, or work activities.

27. Practice with employee communication skills that encourage nonconflictual conversation (e.g., absence of blaming, active listening, nondefensiveness).

28. Assign employee homework of initiating a short conversation with child on a topic that the child chooses.

29. Recommend that employee and spouse set up meeting with school official (e.g., principal, teacher, counselor) to review child's academic situation and behavior and to solicit advice and resources from the school.

30. Assist employee in identifying catastrophic fears and beliefs connected to allowing child increased independent activity.

31. Identify with employee the long-term behavioral consequences (e.g., dependency, separation anxiety, decreased self-sufficiency)

of family emeshment and over-protectiveness.

32. Challenge belief of inevitability of catastrophic outcomes connected to child's independent activity away from employee.

33. Direct employee to allow child a planned, age-appropriate activity away from employee and/or home.

—. _____
   _____

—. _____
   _____

—. _____
   _____

DIAGNOSTIC SUGGESTIONS

Axis I:	296.xx	Major Depressive Disorder
	309.24	Adjustment Disorder With Anxiety
	309.0	Adjustment Disorder With Depressed Mood
	309.3	Adjustment Disorder With Disturbance of Conduct
	309.28	Adjustment Disorder With Mixed Anxiety and Depressed Mood
	309.4	Adjustment Disorder With Mixed Disturbance of Emotions and Conduct
	V61.1	Partner Relational Problem
	V61.1	Physical Abuse of Adult (995.81, Victim)
	V61.20	Parent-Child Relational Problem
	V61.21	Neglect of Child (995.5, Victim)
	V61.21	Physical Abuse of Child (995.5, Victim)
	V61.21	Sexual Abuse of Child (995.5, Victim)
	_____	_____
	_____	
Axis II:	301.6	Dependent Personality Disorder
	_____	_____
	_____	_____

PHOBIA-PANIC/AGORAPHOBIA

BEHAVIORAL DEFINITIONS

1. A persistent and unreasonable fear of a specific object or situation (e.g., flying, riding in an elevator, being near a window in a tall building) that promotes avoidance behaviors that interfere with work.
2. Unexpected, sudden, and repeated panic symptoms (shallow breathing, sweating, heart racing or pounding, dizziness, depersonalization or derealization, trembling, chest tightness, fear of dying or losing control, nausea).
3. Avoidance of such situations as leaving home alone, being in a crowd of people, or traveling in an enclosed environment, because of associated anxiety symptoms.
4. Persistence of fear in spite of recognition that the fear is unreasonable.
5. No evidence of agoraphobia.
6. No evidence of panic disorder.

—. _____
   _____
   _____
—. _____
   _____
   _____
—. _____
   _____

LONG-TERM GOALS

1. Reduce fear so that he/she can independently remain in any work situation and perform tasks essential to the job.
2. Reduce fear so that he/she can independently and freely leave home and comfortably be in public environments.

133

3. Reduce fear of the specific stimulus object or situation that previously provoked immediate anxiety.
4. Eliminate interference in normal work and family routines and remove distress from feared object or situation.
5. Reduce panic symptoms and the fear that they will recur without the ability to cope with and control them.

—. _____
_____
—. _____
_____
—. _____
_____

SHORT-TERM OBJECTIVES

1. End current panic attack and return to work. (1)
2. Provide history of attacks of fear or panic. (2)
3. Verbalize fear and focus on describing the specific stimuli for it. (3, 12, 13)
4. Accept referral for medical examination and medication evaluation. (4)
5. Construct a hierarchy of situations that increasingly evoke anxiety. (5)
6. Begin practice in progressive, deep-muscle relaxation. (6, 7, 8)
7. Identify a nonthreatening pleasant scene that can be utilized to promote relaxation using guided imagery. (8)

THERAPEUTIC INTERVENTIONS

1. Reassure employee that he/she can regain control while focusing him/her on slow, rhythmic breathing, bringing calm to current attack.
2. Solicit history of employee's phobia/panic attacks.
3. Discuss and assess employee's fear, its depth, and the stimuli for it.
4. Refer employee for medical examination to rule out a physical disorder and evaluate for psychotropic medication.
5. Direct and assist employee in construction of hierarchy of anxiety-producing situations.
6. Demonstrate progressive relaxation techniques that teach systematic attention

8. Begin a systematic desensitization program to the anxiety-provoking stimulus object or situation. (8, 9)

9. Undergo in vivo desensitization to the stimulus object or situation. (10)

10. Leave home without overwhelming anxiety. (4, 9, 10, 11, 16)

11. Encounter the phobic stimulus object or situation feeling in control, calm, and comfortable. (3, 10, 11, 16)

12. Identify symbolic significance that the phobic stimulus may have as a basis for fear. (3, 12)

13. Understand the separate realities of the irrationally feared object or situation and the emotionally painful experience from the past that has been evoked by the phobic stimulus. (3, 13, 14, 15)

14. Share the feelings associated with past emotionally painful situation that is connected to the phobia. (12, 13, 14, 15)

15. Differentiate real from distorted, imagined situations that can produce rational and irrational fear. (13, 14, 15, 16)

16. Utilize behavioral and cognitive mechanisms to reduce or eliminate irrational anxiety. (6, 8, 10, 16, 18)

to deep-muscle release of tension.

7. Refer for biofeedback treatment to facilitate relaxation skills.

8. Introduce guided imagery technique that outlines a pleasant, relaxing scene which can be brought to mind for anxiety relief.

9. Suggest systematic desensitization procedures that pair relaxation with the feared stimulus to reduce phobic response.

10. Assign and/or accompany the employee for in vivo desensitization contact with phobic stimulus object or situation.

11. Review and verbally reinforce progress toward overcoming anxiety.

12. Probe, discuss, and interpret possible symbolic meaning of the phobic stimulus object or situation.

13. Clarify and differentiate between the employee's current irrational fear and past emotional pain.

14. Encourage employee to share feelings from past through active listening, positive regard, and questioning.

15. Reinforce employee insights into past emotional pain and present anxiety.

16. Train employee in coping strategies (diversion, deep

17. Verbalize an understanding of the cognitive beliefs and messages that mediate anxiety response. (3, 5, 17, 18)

18. Verbalize positive, healthy, and rational self-talk that reduces fear and allows the behavioral encounter with avoided stimuli. (16, 17, 18)

19. Responsibly take prescribed psychotropic medication to alleviate phobic anxiety. (19)

—. _____
   _____

—. _____
   _____

—. _____
   _____

breathing, positive self-talk, muscle relaxation, etc.) to alleviate symptoms.

17. Identify the employee's distorted schemas and related automatic thoughts that mediate anxiety response.

18. Train employee in revising core schemas using cognitive restructuring techniques.

19. Follow up and verbally reinforce compliance with medication regimen.

—. _____
   _____

—. _____
   _____

—. _____
   _____

DIAGNOSTIC SUGGESTIONS

Axis I: 300.22   Agoraphobia Without History of Panic Disorder
            300.21   Panic Disorder With Agoraphobia
            300.01   Panic Disorder Without Agoraphobia
            300.29   Specific Phobia

            _____   _____
            _____   _____

Axis II: 301.6   Dependent Personality Disorder
            301.4   Obsessive-Compulsive Personality Disorder
            301.9   Personality Disorder NOS

            _____   _____
            _____   _____

PUBLIC SPEAKING ANXIETY

BEHAVIORAL DEFINITIONS

1. History of career setbacks or a career plateau based on a pattern of anxiety, shyness, or timidity which is present in work situations that require verbal communication to an audience of coworkers, management, or customers.
2. Hypersensitivity to perceived criticism or disapproval from a work-related audience.
3. Avoidance of situations that require verbal presentation to a group or audience.
4. Persistent worry about saying or doing something foolish or becoming emotional in front of a work-related group.
5. Abuse of alcohol or other drugs to ease the anxiety connected with speaking to work-related groups.
6. Increased heart rate, sweating, dry mouth, muscle tension, and shakiness when required to speak to work-related groups.

—. _____
_____
—. _____
_____
—. _____
_____

LONG-TERM GOALS

1. Verbally communicate in work-related groups without excessive fear or anxiety.
2. Conceptualize, plan, and execute effective verbal presentations to groups of coworkers, management, or customers.

3. Eliminate interference in career development related to fear of speaking to work-related groups.

—. _____

_____

—. _____

_____

—. _____

_____

SHORT-TERM OBJECTIVES

1. Identify and clarify perceived fears connected to public speaking. (1)

2. Distinguish past experiences of significant performance anxiety in personal history from the present and the future. (2, 3)

3. List and/or describe potential positive outcomes resulting from successful verbal presentations in work-related situations. (4)

4. Accept referral to a physician for examination and antianxiety medication evaluation. (5)

5. Take antianxiety medication as prescribed and report side effects and effectiveness in public speaking engagements. (6)

6. Verbalize distorted cognitions that mediate fear response in public speaking situations. (3, 7)

THERAPEUTIC INTERVENTIONS

1. Assist employee in identifying catastrophic fears and fantasies connected to public speaking situations.

2. Solicit and probe employee's past experiences of disabling anxiety in public speaking.

3. Challenge employee's belief that past experience must determine current outcomes.

4. Ask employee to list potential positive career outcomes related to improvement in public speaking skills.

5. Refer employee for physical examination and evaluation for medication used to reduce anxiety or physiological overarousal.

6. Review employee's understanding of medication use and prescription compliance, monitoring for side effects and effectiveness.

7. Demonstrate understanding of the disabling role irrational cognitions play in increasing and maintaining anxiety. (3, 7, 8)

8. Verbalize a positive self-talk dialogue that decreases anxiety connected to public speaking. (9)

9. Report instances in which increased assertiveness skills were implemented. (10)

10. Practice relaxation and/or self-calming techniques. (11, 12)

11. Increase frequency and length of verbalizations to groups of coworkers, managers, or customers. (13, 14)

12. Verbally describe a plan for a successful verbal presentation to a work-related group. (14, 15, 16)

—. _____
   _____

—. _____
   _____

—. _____
   _____

7. Vigorously challenge employee's distorted belief in the inevitability of catastrophic outcomes connected to public speaking situations.

8. Illustrate for employee the role that irrational cognitions play in the emotional consequences following activating events.

9. Script self-talk dialogue for employee that promotes a rational response to the demands and probable outcomes of the public speaking situation (see *What To Say When You Talk to Yourself,* by Helmstetter).

10. Train employee in assertiveness skills, refer him/her to an assertiveness training class and/or assign the reading of assertiveness books (e.g., *Feel the Fear and Do It Anyway,* by Jeffers).

11. Provide training exercise to demonstrate calming influence of a present focus.

12. Train employee in focused deep breathing, mindfulness, meditation, and/or relaxation skills.

13. Assign employee homework of verbalizing in a staff meeting, group team meeting, union meeting, customer meeting, etc.

14. Ask employee to videotape a short presentation on an assigned subject. Review videotape in employee's

presence and provide con-
structive critique and positive feedback where
appropriate.

15. Review and/or train
employee in outlining skills
necessary for effective written or verbal presentations.

16. Ask employee to rehearse
part or all of an upcoming
presentation in the pres-
ence of the EAP counselor.

—. _____
    _____
—. _____
    _____
—. _____
    _____

DIAGNOSTIC SUGGESTIONS

Axis I:	300.00	Anxiety Disorder NOS
	302.71	Generalized Anxiety Disorder
	296.xx	Major Depressive Disorder
	300.01	Panic Disorder Without Agoraphobia
	300.23	Social Phobia
	300.4	Dysthymic Disorder
	_____	_____
Axis II:	301.0	Paranoid Personality Disorder
	301.9	Personality Disorder NOS
	_____	_____
	_____	_____

SUICIDE RISK

BEHAVIORAL DEFINITIONS

1. Verbalization of thoughts and feelings that reflect a desire to end the strain and pressures of work or home life.
2. Discussions with colleagues about the mounting pressures he/she is experiencing at work or home and the feeling that he/she is not able to cope with them.
3. Actively seeks out colleagues telling them they will be missed and implicitly or explicitly saying good-bye without an explanation of where he/she is going.
4. Talking about a plan for ending his/her life.
5. History of severe and chronic depression coupled with an increase in absenteeism or tardiness.
6. Recurrent references to and discussions about death.
7. Gradual or sudden change of appearance which reflects a lack of personal care and hygiene.
8. Expressions of hopelessness regarding life coupled with recent life events that relate to this attitude, such as interpersonal problems, divorce, death, or job pressures.
9. Withdrawal from usual and customary interaction with colleagues at work.
10. Bouts of crying for no apparent external reason.

___. _____

_____

___. _____

_____

___. _____

_____

LONG-TERM GOALS

1. Alleviate suicidal impulses/ideation and return to previous level of daily functioning.
2. Stabilize suicidal situation and establish community and work-based "signals" that would identify escalating suicidal crisis situations in the future.
3. Refer to and, if possible, motivate his/her acceptance of appropriate level of care to address suicidal crisis and the need for professional assistance.
4. Reestablish a sense of hope.
5. Regain positive feelings about work and acknowledge the importance of the structure it provides.
6. Regain positive feelings about and pleasure derived from various aspects of life.

—. _____

_____

—. _____

_____

—. _____

_____

SHORT-TERM OBJECTIVES

1. Openly verbalize the degree of interest in dying versus living. (1, 4)

2. Identify life factors and precipitating events that preceded the suicidal ideation. (2)

3. Understand and express with appropriate affect, the feelings and thoughts that underlie suicidal ideation. (2)

4. Comply with regularly scheduled appointments for psychotherapy and

THERAPEUTIC INTERVENTIONS

1. If written permission is granted, contact employee's manager to gain an understanding of on-the-job performance expectations, recent functioning, and any recent or past changes.

2. Take a detailed oral history to assess the problems which encompass employee's suicidal ideation, taking into account the extent of ideation, its history, the presence of a primary and

psychopharmacology treatment. (3)

5. Comply with prescribed medication and/or any homework/directives from therapist/physician. (3)

6. Report no longer feeling the impulse/need to take his/her life. (4)

7. Report a decrease in the frequency and intensity of the suicidal ideation. (3, 4)

8. Go to an emergency room if suicidal urge is overwhelming. (5)

9. Identify at least three reasons for wanting to live and the changes that have occurred to make these reasons obvious now. (6, 7, 8)

10. Reestablish a consistent attendance record at work. (8, 9)

11. Reestablish a work routine of regular productivity, cooperative attitude, and usual interest in responsibilities. (9)

12. Identify previous difficulties at work and ask for assistance in finding ways to be productive, minimizing situations that have caused problems in the past. (8, 9)

13. Report that he/she has discussed suicidal feelings, thoughts, and plans with therapist or doctor. (10, 11)

14. Identify positive changes in his/her life that could make life more pleasant. (7, 12)

back-up plan, past suicide attempts, and family history.

3. Refer employee for outpatient treatment if he/she appears to have sufficient control over life-threatening impulses and will sign a no-harm contract.

4. Engage employee in ongoing dialogue to elicit and monitor any suicidal potential on an ongoing basis.

5. If the employee is uncontrollably distraught, notify security, possibly local police, family, and significant others of the imminent danger he/she poses to self. Direct employee and family to an emergency room for a comprehensive emergency evaluation and treatment.

6. Assist employee in developing an awareness of the reasons that led to his/her despondency and suicidal ideation.

7. Assist employee in finding reasons to live and reinforce his/her importance to you, coworkers, employer, and family.

8. Review work situation with employee to evaluate the specific situations that might put him/her at suicidal risk once again.

9. Review work situation with manager prior to employee's full-time return to work, ensuring that job tasks are appropriate and realistic

15. Agree to avoid music, books, or people that consistently portray a negative outlook toward life, and to surround self with optimistic, affirming people, books, and music. (13)

16. Integrate depression-coping strategies into daily routine. (14, 15)

17. No longer withdraw socially but interact with coworkers with some evidence of camaraderie and humor. (16)

18. Agree to contact therapist, doctor, or EAP when unsure of how to deal with recurring suicidal feelings. (15, 17)

—. _____
   _____

—. _____
   _____

—. _____
   _____

and the department staff is briefed on how to interact with employee.

10. Get written permission from employee to contact primary therapist or doctor to coordinate ongoing plan to sustain positive attitude and behavior at work.

11. Upon employee's return to work, confer with prescribing primary physician or therapist regarding employee's mental health status once a week tapering off to every three months after the first three months of a successful readjustment.

12. Assist employee in identifying positive changes (e.g., broaden social network, deepen spiritual commitment, help others, reach out to family, change work responsibilities) that would make his/her life more satisfying.

13. Encourage employee to seek out sources of encouragement, such as upbeat friends, spiritual leaders, and inspiring books and music.

14. Coordinate employee's coping strategies for suicidal ideation (e.g., more physical exercise, less internal focus, increased social involvement, and greater expression of feelings) with prescribing primary physician or therapist.

15. Take the initiative in encouraging and being interested in the employee's adjustment, attitude, and feelings.

16. Encourage and reinforce sociability with coworkers.

17. Inform employee of your continued availability for ongoing support, guidance, and crisis intervention on a regular basis. Initiate these contacts consistently.

___. _____
    _____

___. _____
    _____

___. _____
    _____

DIAGNOSTIC SUGGESTIONS

Axis I: 300.4   Dysthymic Disorder
             296.2x   Major Depressive Disorder, Single Episode
             296.3x   Major Depressive Disorder, Recurrent
             296.xx   Bipolar I Disorder

             _____   _____

Axis II: 301.83   Borderline Personality Disorder

             _____   _____

             _____   _____

THREAT OF VIOLENCE

BEHAVIORAL DEFINITIONS

1. Verbal threats of violence to coworker(s), manager(s), or both.
2. Intimates violence toward coworker(s) or manager(s), either verbally or through behavior.
3. Admits fear of loss of control over impulses to physically assault coworker(s) or manager(s).
4. Consistently broods over perceived injustices in the workplace and speaks about revenge.
5. Fascinated by other workplace violence situations and discusses and personalizes them or collects information about them, intimidating coworkers or managers.
6. Threatens to destroy company equipment or property.

___. _____

_____

___. _____

_____

___. _____

_____

LONG-TERM GOALS

1. Able to significantly decrease chronic feelings of rage and anger that precipitate violent impulses.
2. Able to tolerate legitimate anger without resorting to threats of violence.
3. Decrease fantasies and/or verbal threats of revenge following perceived incidents of injustice.

4. Decrease verbalizations of suspiciousness of coworkers and managers.
5. Increase prosocial behaviors that lead to stronger, supportive relationships with coworkers.

___. _____

_____

_____

___. _____

_____

___. _____

_____

SHORT-TERM OBJECTIVES

1. Agree to interview with EAP. (1)
2. Decrease intensity and frequency of hostile comments during sessions and be able to maintain calm demeanor during sessions. (2)
3. Describe the immediate events that led to threat response in a coherent and nonpsychotic manner. (3, 5, 6)
4. Share history of violent behavior witnessed or initiated by self. (4, 7)
5. Describe previous career functioning, coworker relationships, and conflicts with management. (5, 7)
6. Describe the predicted result of the violence for self, victims, employer, and his/her loved ones. (6, 7)

THERAPEUTIC INTERVENTIONS

1. Recommend to human resources or line manager that employee be seen as soon as possible by EAP.
2. Attempt to calm employee's immediate anger by labeling and accepting feelings of anger, frustration, hurt, etc., while redirecting him/her to more constructive behavioral expressions.
3. Ask employee to explain what led to threat response by describing the event from the point of view of a neutral observer.
4. Solicit through interview employee's history of violence that he/she has perpetrated or witnessed.
5. Explore employee's previous career functioning and depth of interpersonal relationships and conflicts.

7. Accept referral for psychological/psychiatric evaluation. (8)

8. Provide appropriate workplace authorities with relevant information for the purpose of establishing the safety of threatened victims. (9, 10, 11)

9. Agree to treatment recommendations following from psychological/psychiatric evaluation. (12)

10. Verbalize credible assurance that s/he will not act on his/her threats. (13, 14)

11. Verbalize understanding of workplace response to threats of violence. (15, 16)

12. Take responsibility for threat behavior as opposed to blaming others for its perceived inevitability. (17)

13. Identify cognitive distortions that lead to feelings of rage. (18)

14. Verbalize positive self-talk that leads to conflict resolution versus rage. (19)

15. Offer alternatives to threat behavior for these grievances and future, hypothetical, similar situations. (20)

16. Demonstrate self-calming techniques for dealing with possible situations of perceived injustices in the future. (21, 22)

17. Demonstrate the ability to depersonalize perceived

6. Ask employee to explain what the fantasized aftermath of a violent act would be versus the probable outcome for him/herself, the victims of the threat, the corporation, and his/her loved ones.

7. Assess employee's emotional stability in terms of ability to control anger and remain nonviolent.

8. Refer employee for psychiatric evaluation with respect to his/her degree of dangerousness.

9. Inform workplace security, management, and/or HR of employee's referral for further evaluation and of his/her threat to the welfare of others.

10. Convene/notify violence prevention committee if one exists at workplace.

11. Set up contingency plan with workplace security, manager, and/or HR to respond to employee's unauthorized return to the workplace.

12. Monitor and evaluate compliance with and effectiveness of psychological treatment in decreasing employee's degree of dangerousness.

13. Ask employee if he/she plans to follow through with threat of violence. Contact workplace security and/or

injustices by discussing them in a context of corporate culture, change, or policy. (23, 24)

18. Offer apology to appropriate coworkers and/or managers. (25)

19. Answer questions from coworkers about the violence threat or his/her associated absence. (26)

20. Agree to follow-up visits with the EAP counselor. (27)

—. _____

_____

—. _____

_____

—. _____

_____

police immediately if threat appears real.

14. Ask employee to explain why he/she has rescinded threat of violence.

15. Help employee understand workplace rules regarding threats of violence.

16. Contact human resources manager to secure copy of workplace violence policy and share policy with employee.

17. Confront employee with his/her blame of others and avoidance of responsibility for choosing threat behavior as a response to a perceived wrong.

18. Teach employee that arbitrary, selective, black-and-white thinking can lead to hostile emotions.

19. Ask employee to suggest alternative self-dialogue for situations that have led to his/her reactive feelings of revenge and hostility.

20. Ask employee to list alternative responses to violence for redressing perceived grievance.

21. Demonstrate and model for employee self-dialogue that reduces strong negative emotional states.

22. Demonstrate and model relaxation techniques.

23. Discuss and debate with employee irrational entitlements or persecutory

ideation connected with stressful workplace events, attempting to establish a more realistic perspective.

24. Model for employee alternative beliefs to irrational entitlements or persecutory ideation that place unfavorable workplace events in a wider framework (e.g., corporate culture and/or current economic forces).

25. Review with employee appropriate coworkers or managers to whom he/she should apologize.

26. Review and role-play with employee answers to hypothetical questions that coworkers may ask about the cause of his/her absence.

27. Solicit agreement from employee for follow-up EAP visit.

___. _____

_____

___. _____

_____

___. _____

_____

DIAGNOSTIC SUGGESTIONS

Axis I:

296.xx	Bipolar I Disorder
296.89	Bipolar II Disorder
298.8	Brief Psychotic Disorder
297.1	Delusional Disorder
295.7	Schizoaffective Disorder

	295.xx	Schizophrenia
	295.30	Schizophrenia, Paranoid Type
	296.xx	Major Depressive Disorder
	310.1	Personality Change Due to [Axis III Disorder]
	V21.01	Adult Antisocial Behavior
	_____	_____
	_____	_____
Axis II:	301.83	Borderline Personality Disorder
	301.22	Schizotypal Personality Disorder
	301.2	Antisocial Personality Disorder
	301.9	Personality Disorder NOS
	_____	_____
	_____	_____

WORK-FAMILY BALANCE

BEHAVIORAL DEFINITIONS

1. Complaints of confusion and indecision connected to competing demands on time from job and family.
2. Fear regarding impending, or already incurred, job disciplinary measures due to absenteeism or tardiness stemming from family responsibilities.
3. Decreased productivity at work resulting from anxious or depressive feelings connected to caring for a dependent (invalid, child, or aged adult) family member.
4. Reports of difficulty in finding resources to aid in the care of a dependent family member.
5. Feelings of incompetence or guilt as a parent or a caregiver connected with perceived lack of time spent caring for dependent family member.

__. _____
   _____
   _____
__. _____
   _____
   _____
__. _____
   _____

LONG-TERM GOALS

1. Establishment of a balanced response to demands from work and family.
2. Selection of and satisfaction with dependent-care resource(s).

3. Ability to work productively without undue worry connected to care for dependent family members.
4. Minimal absenteeism or tardiness stemming from family responsibilities.
5. Realistic perspective on the importance of career achievement in relation to family responsibilities.

—. _____

_____

—. _____

_____

—. _____

_____

SHORT-TERM OBJECTIVES

1. Describe nature of conflicts between family and workplace responsibilities. (1, 2, 3)

2. Review previous attempts at solving conflicting work-family demands. (4, 12)

3. Explain and evaluate career goal(s) in relation to demands from family responsibilities. (5, 6)

4. Investigate workplace-sponsored responses to work-family issues (e.g, flex time, alternate shift work, job sharing) and list the pros and cons for his/her family situation. (7, 8)

5. Investigate corporate-, union-, or community-sponsored care for dependent family member(s). (7, 8, 9, 10, 11)

THERAPEUTIC INTERVENTIONS

1. Actively listen to employee's story regarding stress emanating from work-family conflict.

2. Solicit employee's worries and fears about effects of current situation on self, family, and career.

3. Challenge employee to present work-family conflict as objectively as possible.

4. Ask employee to list previous attempts at solving work-family conflict.

5. Have employee discuss career goals, both mid- and long-term.

6. Challenge employee's tendency to substitute preferences and desires for "musts" connected with work and family goals.

6. Meet with human resources or line manager to gain approval for workplace accommodation to meet family responsibilities. (8)

7. Identify sources of support from extended family and significant friends which could lessen burden of caring for dependent family member(s). (10, 11, 12, 13)

8. Hold meeting with spouse/significant other to evaluate possible mutual solutions to work-family imbalance (including changing jobs, reducing employment status from full-time to part-time, changing shifts). (14, 15)

9. Select a care provider for dependent family member. (16)

10. Decrease verbalizations reflecting feelings of hopelessness and either/or thinking connected to work-family conflict. (17, 18, 19)

11. Determine financial impact of decreasing work hours or leaving job. (20)

12. Initiate search for more "family-friendly" job. (21)

13. Verbalize a decrease in ruminative worries about the safety or condition of dependent family member(s) while at work. (22, 23)

14. Demonstrate a reduction in negative self-statements regarding parenting or caregiving abilities. (24)

7. Ask employee to contact human resources manager to review corporate-sponsored responses to work-family conflict (e.g., job sharing, flex time, corporate sponsored or discounted day-care program).

8. Plan with employee a meeting to be held with manager to work out specific accommodation to work-family conflict.

9. Assist employee in finding dependent-care resources sponsored by the community, the corporation, or the union.

10. Plan and review employee's contacts with and interviews of care providers for dependent family members.

11. Solicit employee's views of different child-care models (e.g., in-home care vs. outside-home program).

12. Solicit employee's past experience and/or current feelings connected with asking family or close friend for help with care of dependent family member.

13. Discuss fair reimbursement system for family or close friend providing help with care of dependent family member to avoid building resentment in relationship or feelings of guilt in employee.

14. Solicit employee's past experience and/or current

___. _____

     _____

___. _____

     _____

___. _____

     _____

feelings connected with discussing job change with spouse/significant other that could result in lower income and/or different work hours but increased time for family.

15. Set up conjoint meeting with spouse/significant other to discuss job changes to decrease work-family conflict.

16. Construct rating list of advantages and disadvantages connected with dependent family member care possibilities.

17. Solicit and process with employee evidence of stress-increasing cognitions regarding work-family conflict that include rigid, either/or solutions to the work-family balance, and good/bad self-views connected to career role and caregiver role.

18. Demonstrate for employee how irrational, black-white thinking and overgeneralizations lead to emotions that are disruptive and increase stress connected to work-family conflict.

19. Model for employee rational self-statements that allow for compromise in career role and caregiver role.

20. Ask employee to calculate what decreased wages from decreased work hours (i.e., connected with part-time

work or less-demanding job) will mean to family budget.

21. Review plans for and progress with job search for job that will decrease conflict between work and family responsibilities.

22. Solicit, explain, and challenge employee's catastrophizing cognitions regarding the condition of dependent family member while employee is at work that lead to employee's emotional distress and decreased job performance.

23. Demonstrate how replacing catastrophizing cognitions with rational self-talk about the condition of the dependent family member can decrease disabling emotions that interfere with work.

24. Solicit, explain, and challenge employee's negative self-statements that lead to feelings of guilt, low self-esteem, and decreased work, parenting, or caregiving efficiency.

—. _____

_____

—. _____

_____

—. _____

_____

DIAGNOSTIC SUGGESTIONS

Axis I:	309.28	Adjustment Disorder With Mixed Anxiety and Depressed Mood
	309.0	Adjustment Disorder With Depressed Mood
	300.4	Dysthymic Disorder
	301.4	Occupational Problem
	_____	_____
	_____	_____

Appendix A

BIBLIOTHERAPY SUGGESTIONS

Abusive Partner

Bach, G., and Wyden, P. (1976). *The Intimate Enemy: How to Fight Fair in Love and Marriage*. New York: Avon Books.

Fisher, B. (1981). *ReBuilding: When Your Relationship Ends*. San Luis Obispo, CA: Impact.

Fromm, E. (1956). *The Art of Loving*. New York: Harper & Row.

Gorski, T. (1993). *Getting Love Right: Learning the Choices of Healthy Intimacy*. New York: Simon & Schuster.

Gray, J. (1993). *Men and Women and Relationships: Making Peace with the Opposite Sex*. Hillsboro, OR: Beyond Words.

Harley, W. (1994). *His Needs, Her Needs: Building an Affair-Proof Marriage*. Grand Rapids, MI: Revell.

Lerner, H. (1989). *The Dance of Intimacy: A Woman's Guide to Courageous Acts of Change in Key Relationships*. New York: Harper Perennial.

Lindbergh, A. (1955). *A Gift from the Sea*. New York: Pantheon.

Loring, M. (1997). *Emotional Abuse*. New York: Jossey Bass.

Anger Management

Ellis, A. (1977). *Anger: How to Live With and Without It*. Secaucus, NJ: Citadel Press.

Lerner, H. (1985). *The Dance of Anger: A Woman's Guide to Changing the Patterns of Intimate Relationships*. New York: Harper Perennial.

McKay, M.; Rogers, P.; and McKay, J. (1989). *When Anger Hurts*. Oakland, CA: New Harbinger.

Rosellini, G., and Worden, M. (1986). *Of Course You're Angry*. San Francisco: Harper Hazelden.

Rubin, T. I. (1969). *The Angry Book.* New York: Macmillan.

Smedes, L. (1991). *Forgive and Forget: Healing the Hurts We Don't Deserve.* San Francisco: Harper.

Tavris, C. (1989). *Anger: The Misunderstood Emotion.* New York: Touchstone Books.

Antisocial Behavior

Carnes, Patrick (1983). *Out of the Shadows: Understanding Sexual Addictions.* Minneapolis, MN: CompCare.

Katherine, A. (1991). *Boundaries: Where You End and I Begin.* New York: Simon & Schuster.

Williams, R., and Williams, V. (1993). *Anger Kills.* New York: Time Books.

Chemical Dependence

Alcoholics Anonymous (1975). *Living Sober.* New York: A. A. World Service.

Alcoholics Anonymous (1976). *Alcoholics Anonymous: The Big Book.* New York: A. A. World Service.

Carnes, P. (1989). *A Gentle Path Through the Twelve Steps.* Minneapolis, MN: CompCare.

Clemmens, M. (1996). *Getting Beyond Sobriety.* New York: Jossey Bass.

Drews, T. R. (1980). *Getting Them Sober: A Guide for Those Living with Alcoholism.* South Plainfield, NJ: Bridge Publishing.

Johnson, V. (1980). *I'll Quit Tomorrow.* New York: Harper & Row.

Nuckals, C. (1989). *Cocaine: From Dependence to Recovery.* Blue Ridge Summit, PA: TAB Books.

Wilson, B. (1967). *As Bill Sees It.* New York: A. A. World Service.

Chemical Dependence Relapse

Alcoholics Anonymous (1975). *Living Sober.* New York: A. A. World Service.

Alcoholics Anonymous (1976). *Alcoholics Anonymous: The Big Book.* New York: A. A. World Service.

Carnes, P. (1989). *A Gentle Path Through the Twelve Steps.* Minneapolis, MN: CompCare Publishing.

Drews, T. R. (1980). *Getting Them Sober: A Guide for Those Living with Alcoholism.* South Plainfield, NJ: Bridge Publishing.

Gorski, T., and Miller, M. (1986). *Staying Sober: A Guide to Relapse Prevention.* Independence, MO: Herald House Press.

Gorski, T. (1989–92). *The Staying Sober Workbook.* Independence, MO: Herald House Press.

Johnson, V. (1980). *I'll Quit Tomorrow.* New York: Harper & Row.

Larson, E. (1985). *Stage II Recovery: Life Beyond Addiction.* San Francisco, CA: Harper & Row.

Nuckals, C. (1989). *Cocaine: From Dependency to Recovery.* Blue Ridge Summit, PA: TAB Books.

Wilson, B. (1967). *As Bill Sees It.* New York: A. A. World Service.

Depression

Burns, D. (1980). *Feeling Good: The New Mood Therapy.* New York: Signet.

Burns, D. (1989). *The Feeling Good Handbook.* New York: Plume.

Dyer, W. (1974). *Your Erroneous Zones.* New York: Funk & Wagnalls.

Frankl, V. (1959). *Man's Search for Meaning.* New York: Simon & Schuster.

Geisel, T. (1990). *Oh, The Places You'll Go.* New York: Random House.

Greist, John, M.D. and Jefferson, James, M.D. (1992). *Depression and Its Treatment.* New York: Warner Books.

Hallinan, P. K. (1976). *One Day at a Time.* Minneapolis, MN: CompCare.

Hazelden Staff (1991). *Each Day a New Beginning.* Center City, MN: Hazelden.

Knauth, P. (1977). *A Season in Hell.* New York: Pocket Books.

Disciplinary Stress

Bolles, R. (1992). *What Color Is Your Parachute?* Berkeley, CA: Ten-Speed Press.

Charland, R. (1993). *Career Shifting: Starting Over in a Changing Economy.* Holbrook, MA: Bob Adams.

Fisher, Roger and Brown, Scott (1988). *Getting Together.* New York: Penguin Books.

Jandt, F. (1985). *Win-Win Negotiating: Turning Conflict into Agreement.* New York: John Wiley & Sons.

Weiss, R. (1990). *Staying the Course: The Emotional and Social Lives of Men Who Do Well at Work.* New York: Free Press.

Eating Disorder

Hollis, J. (1985). *Fat Is a Family Affair.* New York: Harper & Row.

Sherman, Roberta T. (1996). *Bulimia.* New York: Jossey Bass.

Educational Deficits

de Boro, E. (1982). *de Boro's Thinking Course.* New York: Facts of Life Publishing.

Sandstrom, R. (1990). *The Ultimate Memory Book.* Granada, CA: Stepping Stones Books.

Gambling

Lesier, H. (1993). *Understanding Compulsive Gambling*. Center City, Minnesota: Hazelden.

Gowan, W. D. (1988). *Early Signs of Compulsive Gambling*. Center City, Minnesota: Hazelden.

Lorenz, V. (1988). *Releasing Guilt About Gambling*. Center City, Minnesota: Hazelden.

Heineman, M. (1988). *When Someone You Love Gambles*. Center City, Minnesota: Hazelden.

Grief/Loss

Colgrove, M. (1991). *How to Survive the Loss of a Love*. Los Angeles: Prelude Press.

Kushner, H. (1981). *When Bad Things Happen to Good People*. New York: Schocken Books.

Lewis, C. S. (1961). *A Grief Observed*. New York: The Seabury Press.

Rando, T. (1991). *How to Go on Living When Someone You Love Dies*. New York: Bantam.

Schiff, N. (1977). *The Bereaved Parent*. New York: Crown Publication.

Smedes, L. (1982). *How Can It Be All Right When Everything Is All Wrong*. San Francisco: Harper.

Westberg, G. (1962). *Good Grief*. Philadelphia: Augsburg Fortress Press.

Wolterstorff, N. (1987). *Lament for a Son*. Grand Rapids, MI: Eerdmans.

Legal Conflicts

Carnes, P. (1983). *Out of the Shadows: Understanding Sexual Addictions*. Minneapolis, MN: CompCare.

Williams, R., and Williams, V. (1993). *Anger Kills*. New York: Time Books.

Low Self-Esteem

Burns, D. (1993). *Ten Days to Self Esteem!* New York: William Morrow.

Helmstetter, S. (1986). *What to Say When You Talk to Yourself*. New York: Fine Communications.

McKay, M., and Fanning, P. (1987). *Self-Esteem*. Oakland, CA: New Harbinger.

Managerial Deficiencies

Spencer, I. and Spencer, P. (1993). *Competence at Work: Models for Superior Performance*. New York: John Wiley & Son.

Block, P. (1987). *The Empowered Manager.* San Francisco, CA: Jossey Bass Publishers.

Medical Problem

Friedman, M., and Ulmer, P. (1984). *Treating Type A Behavior and Your Heart.* New York: Alfred Knopf.

Parent-Child Conflict

Bloomfield, H., and Felder, L. (1983). *Making Peace with Your Parents.* New York: Random House.
Faber, A., and Mazlish, E. (1987). *Siblings Without Rivalry.* New York: Norton.
Ginott, H. (1969). *Between Parent and Child.* New York: Macmillan.
Steinberg, L., and Levine, A. (1990). *You and Your Adolescent: A Parents' Guide for Ages 10–20.* New York: Harper Perennial.

Phobia-Panic/Agoraphobia

Gold, M. (1988). *The Good News About Panic, Anxiety, and Phobias.* New York: Villard/Random House.
Marks, I. (1980). *Living with Fear: Understanding and Coping with Anxiety.* New York: McGraw-Hill.
Swede, S., and Jaffe, S. (1987). *The Panic Attack Recovery Book.* New York: New American Library.
Wilson, R. (1986). *Don't Panic: Taking Control of Anxiety Attacks.* New York: Harper & Row.

Public Speaking Anxiety

Benson, H. (1975). *The Relaxation Response.* New York: William Morrow.
Davis, M., Eshelman, E., and McKay, M. (1988). *The Relaxation and Stress Reduction Workbook.* Oakland, CA: New Harbinger.
Hauck, Paul (1975). *Overcoming Worry and Fear.* Philadelphia, PA: Westminster Press.
Jeffers, S. (1987). *Feel the Fear and Do It Anyway.* San Diego, CA: Harcourt Brace Jovanovich.
Marks, Issac (1980). *Living with Fear: Understanding and Coping with Anxiety.* New York: McGraw-Hill.

Suicide Risk

Butler, P. (1991). *Talking to Yourself: Learning the Language of Self-Affirmation.* New York: Stein and Day.
Hutschnecker, A. (1951). *The Will to Live.* New York: Cornerstone Library.
Seligman, M. (1990). *Learned Optimism: The Skill to Conquer Life's Obstacles, Large and Small.* New York: Pocket Books.

Work-Family Balance

Friedman, D., Rimsky, C., and Johnson, A. (1993). *The Changing Workforce: Highlights from the National Study.* New York: Family and Work Institute.
Shinn, M., Galinsky, E., and Guleur, L. (1990). *The Changing Employer-Employee Contract: The Role of Work-Family Issues.* New York: Family and Work Institute.

Appendix B

INDEX OF DSM-IV CODES ASSOCIATED WITH PRESENTING PROBLEMS

Alcohol Dependence   303.90
  Antisocial Behavior
  Chemical Dependence
  Financial Stress
  Medical Problem

Alcohol Intoxication   303.00
  Chemical Dependence Relapse

Antisocial Personality Disorder
                            301.7
  Anger Management
  Antisocial Behavior
  Chemical Dependence
  Chemical Dependence Relapse
  Financial Stress
  Gambling
  Legal Conflicts
  Low Self-Esteem
  Manager Role Conflict
  Managerial Conflict
  Managerial Deficiencies
  Threat of Violence

Anxiety Disorder NOS   300.00
  Anxiety/Panic
  Public Speaking Anxiety

Avoidant Personality Disorder
                            301.82
  Anxiety/Panic

Bereavement   V62.82
  Grief/Loss

Bipolar I Disorder   296.xx
  Anger Management
  Depression
  Suicide Risk
  Threat of Violence

Bipolar I Disorder, Single Manic Episode   296.0x
  Financial Stress

Bipolar II Disorder   296.89
  Anger Management
  Depression
  Threat of Violence

Borderline Intellectual Functioning
                            V62.89
  Educational Deficits

Borderline Personality Disorder
                            301.83
  Abusive Partner
  Anger Management
  Legal Conflict
  Low Self-Esteem
  Managerial Conflict
  Managerial Deficiencies
  Suicide Risk
  Threat of Violence

Brief Psychotic Disorder   298.8
  Threat of Violence

Cannabis Abuse   305.20
  Chemical Dependence
  Chemical Dependence—Relapse

Cannabis Dependence   304.30
  Chemical Dependence
  Financial Stress

Cocaine Dependence   304.20
  Antisocial Behavior
  Chemical Dependence
  Medical Problem

Conduct Disorder   312.8
  Anger Management
  Legal Conflicts
  Managerial Conflict

Delusional Disorder   297.1
  Threat of Violence

Dependent Personality Disorder
                            301.6
  Parent-Child Conflict
  Phobia-Panic/Agoraphobia

Diagnosis Deferred on Axis II   799.9
  Abusive Partner

Disorder of Written Expression
                            315.2
  Educational Deficits

Dysthymic Disorder   300.4
  Depression
  Low Self-Esteem
  Manager Role Conflict
  Managerial Conflict
  Suicide Risk

Eating Disorder NOS   307.50
   Eating Disorder

Generalized Anxiety Disorder
                                 300.02
   Anxiety/Panic
   Public Speaking Anxiety

Hypochondriasis   300.7
   Medical Problem

Identity Problem   313.82
   Coworker conflict
   Managerial Deficiencies

Inhalant Dependence   304.60

Intermittent Explosive Disorder
                                 312.34
   Anger Management
   Antisocial Behavior
   Critical Incident
   Managerial Conflict

Major Depressive Disorder   296.xx
   Low Self-Esteem
   Parent-Child Conflict
   Public Speaking Anxiety
   Threat of Violence

Major Depressive Disorder, Recurrent   296.3x
   Grief/Loss
   Suicide Risk

Major Depressive Disorder, Single Episode   296.2x
   Grief/Loss
   Suicide Risk

Maladaptive Health Behaviors Affecting (*Axis III Disorder*)   316
   Medical Problem

Mild Mental Retardation   317
   Educational Deficits

Narcissistic Personality Disorder
                                 301.81
   Anger Management
   Antisocial Behavior
   Financial Stress

   Manager Role Conflict
   Managerial Conflict
   Marital Conflict

Neglect of a Child   V61.21
                         (995.5, Victim)
   Parent-Child Conflict

No Diagnosis on Axis II   V71.09
   Abusive Partner

Obsessive-Compulsive Personality Disorder   301.4
   Eating Disorder
   Gambling
   Phobia-Panic/Agoraphobia

Occupational Problem   V62.2
   Disciplinary Stress
   Educational Deficits
   Financial Stress

Oppositional Defiant Disorder
                                 313.81
   Legal Conflicts

Pain Disorder Associated With Psychological Factors   307.8
   Medical Problem

Pain Disorder Associated With Both Psychological Factors and (*Axis III Disorder*)   307.89
   Medical Problem

Panic Disorder with Agoraphobia
                                 300.21
   Anxiety/Panic
   Phobia-Panic/Agoraphobia
   Public Speaking Anxiety

Panic Disorder without Agoraphobia   300.01
   Anxiety/Panic
   Phobia-Panic/Agoraphobia
   Public Speaking Anxiety

Paranoid Personality Disorder
                                 301.0
   Antisocial Behavior
   Anger Management
   Coworker Conflict
   Managerial Conflict
   Public Speaking Anxiety

TheraScribe® 3.0 for Windows®

The Computerized Assistant to Psychotherapy Treatment Planning

Spend More Time on Patients - Not Paperwork

→ Used in thousands of behavioral health practices and treatment facilities, *TheraScribe® 3.0* is a state-of-the-art Windows®-based treatment planning program which rapidly generates comprehensive treatment plans meeting the requirements of all major accrediting agencies and most third-party payers.

→ In just minutes, this user-friendly program enables you to create customized treatment plans by choosing from thousands of prewritten built-in short-term goals, long-term objectives, therapeutic interventions, automated progress notes, and much more.

→ This networkable software also tracks treatment outcome, stores clinical pathways, and provides ample room for narrative patient histories, treatment summaries, and discharge notes.

→ And best of all, this flexible system can be expanded to include the data in this *Employee Assistance (EAP) Treatment Planner.*

✎EMPLOYEE ASSISTANCE (EAP) Upgrade to THERASCRIBE 3.0⚓

The behavioral definitions, goals, objectives, and interventions from this *Employee Assistance Treatment Planner* can be imported into *TheraScribe 3.0: The Computerized Assistant to Treatment Planning.* For purchase and pricing information, please send in the coupon below.

— —

For more information about *TheraScribe® 3.0* or the *Employee Assistance (EAP) Upgrade,* fill in this coupon, and mail it to: M. Fellin, John Wiley & Sons, Inc., 605 Third Avenue, New York, NY 10158

❑ Please send me information on TheraScribe® 3.0
❑ Please send me information on the Employee Assistance (EAP) Upgrade to TheraScribe® 3.0

Name _____

Affiliation _____

Address _____

City/State/Zip _____

Phone _____

 WILEY Publishers Since 1807

Build your Treatment Planning Library with these time-saving resources from John Wiley & Sons:

✳ **The Complete Psychotherapy Treatment Planner (adult disorders)**
176pp ◆ Paper ◆ 0471-11738-2 ◆ $39.95

✳ **The Child and Adolescent Psychotherapy Treatment Planner**
240pp ◆ Paper ◆ 0471-15647-7 ◆ $39.95

✳ **The Continuum of Care Treatment Planner**
208pp ◆ Paper ◆ 0471-19568-5 ◆ $39.95

✳ **The Couples Therapy Treatment Planner**
208pp ◆ Paper ◆ 0471-24711-1 ◆ $39.95

✳ **The Chemical Dependence Treatment Planner**
208pp ◆ Paper ◆ 0471-23795-7 ◆ $39.95

✳ **The Pastoral Counseling Therapy Treatment Planner**
208pp ◆ Paper ◆ 0471-25416-9 ◆ $39.95

✳ **TheraScribe® 3.0 for Windows®: *The Computerized Assistant to Psychotherapy Treatment Planning***
Single User/0471-18415-2 ◆ $450.00
Network/0471-18416-0 ◆ Call 1-800-0655 (x4708) for pricing

✳ **TheraBiller w/TheraScheduler™: *The Computerized Mental Health Office Manager***
Single User/0471-17102-2 ◆ $599.95
Network, Call 1-800-0655 (x4708) for pricing

Order the above products through your local bookseller, or by calling
1-800-225-5945 from 8:30 a.m. to 5:30 p.m., est.
Or visit our web site: www.wiley.com/therascribe

For more information about on all of our **PRACTICE PLANNERS™** resources, fill in this coupon, and mail it to: M. Fellin, John Wiley & Sons, Inc., 605 Third Avenue, New York, NY 10158.

Please send me information on:
❑ The Complete Psychotherapy Treatment Planner (adult disorders)
❑ The Child & Adolescent Treatment Planner
❑ The Chemical Dependence Treatment Planner
❑ The Couples Therapy Treatment Planner
❑ The Pastoral Counseling Treatment Planner
❑ The Continuum of Care Treatment Planner
❑ The Group Therapy Treatment Planner
❑ The Older Adult Treatment Psychotherapy Treatment Planner
❑ TheraScribe 3.0
❑ TheraBiller w/TheraScheduler

Name _____
Affiliation _____
Address _____
_____
City/State/Zip _____
Phone _____

WILEY

TheraBiller with TheraScheduler™

The Computerized Mental Health Office Manager

TheraBiller w/TheraScheduler™ is our new Windows®-based software package designed specifically to help you manage your mental health practice....

Powerful...
- TheraBiller™ with TheraScheduler™ integrates seamlessly with TheraScribe® 3.0: The Computerized Assistant to Psychotherapy Treatment Planning. Although each program can be used independently, by using them in cooperatively you'll get a complete office management system, with automatic common data sharing and one-button toggling
- Completes pre-printed or program-generated HCFA forms, and produces easy-to-read, professional-looking invoices and aged accounts receivable reports
- Tracks managed care information (sessions authorized, sessions used, capitated fees, hourly fees, etc.)
- Built-in electronic billing compatibility (claims module interfaces with InStream Provider Network™ or MedE America™ for on-line commerce)
- Electronic cardex which prints mailing labels and tracks contact information

Flexible...
- Robust reporting options — print or preview billing summaries and usage statistics by provider, patient, or time-frame
- Full quick-reference DSM-IV and CPT code libraries (including new G-codes)
- Data export to Quicken® and MicroSoft Money®, as well as common spreadsheet and accounting programs (e.g., Excel®, Peachtree®, etc.)
- Perfect for solo providers or large group practices (the stand-alone version handles an unlimited number of providers, and a network version is also available)

User-Friendly...
- Features the same intuitive interface as Wiley's best-selling TheraScribe ®3.0.
- Includes a handy Billing Wizard to guide you through the billing process and a Report Wizard that helps you select report parameters
- Built-in appointment book, with daily, weekly, monthly scheduling for an unlimited number of providers— updates automatically when you book a session in TheraScribe® 3.0
- Password-protected to safeguard confidential data. Varying levels of data access may be assigned to each user

---

System Requirements
**IBM®-compatible 486DX * 8 MB RAM (12MB recommended) * 10MB Hard Disk Space
VGA display (SVGA recommended) * Windows® 3.1**

For more information on TheraBiller™, fill in this coupon, and mail it to: M. Fellin, John Wiley & Sons, Inc., 605 Third Avenue, New York, NY 10158.

Name _____

Affiliation _____

Address _____

City/State/Zip _____

Phone _____

Visit our web site and download a free demo: www.wiley.com/therabiller

 WILEY *Publishers Since 1807*

ABOUT THE DISK*

TheraScribe® 3.0 Library Module Installation

The enclosed disk contains files to upgrade your TheraScribe® 3.0 program to include the behavioral definitions, goals, objectives, interventions, and diagnoses from *The Employee Assistance Treatment Planner.*

Note: You must have TheraScribe® 3.0 for Windows installed on your computer in order to use *The Employee Assistance Treatment Planner* library module.

To install the library module, please follow these steps:

1. Place the library module disk in your floppy drive.

2. Log in to TheraScribe® 3.0 as the Administrator using the name "Admin" and your administrator password.

3. On the Main Menu, press the "GoTo" button and choose the Options menu item.

4. Press the "Import Library" button.

5. On the Import Library Module screen, choose your floppy disk drive a:\ from the list and press "Go." Note: It may take a few minutes to import the data from the floppy disk to your computer's hard disk.

6. When the installation is complete the library module data will be available in your TheraScribe® 3.0 program.

---

* Note: This section applies only to the book with disk edition, ISBN 0-471-24730-8.

Note: If you have a network version of TheraScribe® 3.0 installed, you should import the library module one time only. After importing the data, the library module data will be available to all network users.

User Assistance

If you need assistance using this TheraScribe® 3.0 add-on module, contact Wiley Technical Support at:

Phone: 212-850-6753
Fax: 212-850-6800 (Attention: Wiley Technical Support)
Email: techhelp@wiley.com

For information on how to install disk, refer to the **About the Disk** section on page 175.

WILEY

Publishers Since 1807

* Note: This section applies only to the book with disk edition, ISBN 0-471-24730-8.